BEST FRIENDS BEST LOVERS

BEST FRIENDS BEST LOVERS

BOB & AUDREY MEISNER

MILESTONES
INTERNATIONAL PUBLISHERS

BEST FRIENDS, BEST LOVERS: Eight Ways to Become Irresistible to Your Spouse

ISBN 0-924748-71-0
UPC 88571300041-3

Printed in the United States of America
© 2006 by Robert and Audrey Meisner
www.bobandaudrey.com

Milestones International Publishers
140 Danika Drive NW
Huntsville, AL 35806
(256) 830-0362; Fax: (256) 830-9206

www.milestonesintl.com

Cover design by Steven Plummer, idesignhomepage.com
Cover image by Getty Images

1 2 3 4 5 6 7 8 9 10 11 / 09 08 07 06

DEDICATION

To the one holding this book...
May your heart be satisfied and your dreams ignited.
It's a day of new beginnings.

***

To Our Future Generations...
May you be given the opportunity to see
the transforming power of God
displayed in our marriage. We do this for you.
Love, Dad and Mom

ACKNOWLEDGMENTS

We are truly grateful for the gift of God's grace in our lives. He has always known exactly what we needed in our journey to personally experience His light, life and love in our hearts. His extravagant and intimate love for us is unending. We can't wait for eternity in Your presence!

Christopher, Janelle, David and Robert
Our four children are the love of our lives. Your joy in the journey, enthusiasm for life, sacrifice for the high calling and your willingness to serve does not go unnoticed. Not to mention that every single one of you is uniquely amazing! We love living with you, laughing with you, praying with you and being with you. Our prayer is that you will experience a life of being satisfied in God, where His life and purposes flow through you like a never-ending river of Grace.

Willard and Betty Thiessen, Audrey's parents:
You have cheered us on and allowed us to escape the box of normality. Your unconditional love for each other and for us is astounding.

Our New Day Ministries Staff:
Without having you in our corner praying for us and fighting for us, this would truly be impossible. And together we will reach multitudes!

Tommy Barnett:
Our pastor who ignites our passion continually, you are a shining of example of what it means to live to give. Your energy and outrageous love for others is contagious...but we love being your favorites!

Dr. James B. Richards:
A wise and trusted teacher who has challenged us, then led us to the heart of God. Thank you for your transparency and openness! You and Brenda are precious friends.

Leo & Molly Godzich:
Our faithful friends who continually war on our behalf and speak inspiration and vision for marriages. Let's live close by each other forever!

Craig & Jan Hill:
Thank you for your impartation and believing in us and giving us opportunity to minister God's grace. I wonder if the Meisner's are up yet?

Gerry and Jan:
You are a shining example of *Best Friends and Best Lovers*. We'll always cherish our friendship with you...memories to last a lifetime.

Phoenix Girls:
We are dynamic and going places grounded in the deep stuff of the Lord. You're a gift to me, and I'm forever grateful. – Audrey

Jim Rill of Milestones Publishers:
You foresee the books in us and make it happen. You're unstoppable. No, really...(I owe you a chicken wing. – Bob)

After ten years of marriage we continued our education with the University of the Nations, YWAM. The rich deposits given in that season of our life, and the cherished relationships have influenced the well of understanding and revelation in our hearts.

We would like to thank the married couples who have inspired this book. Some are friends, others are strangers, but we see you wherever we go. We see you catch each other's eye when it seems nobody is looking. You whisper secrets in each other's ears and break into laughter. You rub shoulders and arms and exchange electric conversation. Thank you for giving us hope that married couples can be everything they dreamed they would be: *Best Friends and Best Lovers*.

FOREWORD

When Bob and Audrey entered the doors of Phoenix First Assembly, they were ministers of the faith who were heartbroken, full of pain, and in great need of a demonstration of God's unconditional love. It was only a short time after the betrayal had been confessed. Audrey was just a few months pregnant, and this family needed a house and a job; but mostly they needed a church family to love them and a place to call home.

I personally watched them receive God's grace right in front of my eyes. I observed them in times of worship and witnessed the powerful presence of God reach into their hearts. I heard about the miracles that enabled them to become a family of strength and influence. The radiance of God's glory transformed them from people of pain to people of passion!

The saddest people in the world are those to whom God gave a plan that they failed to implement for Him. God laid something before them, and they refused to grasp His plan and purpose. Potential requires commitment, sacrifice and work. How sad when someone turns from their potential, believing the price to be too high and the sacrifice too great. God's potential will come to you as a gift. With this potential, God gives a plan, a promise and power. It's never too late!

Best Friends, Best Lovers will entice you to have a marriage beyond the ordinary. You can return to the incredible joy, enthusiasm and passion for your spouse that you dreamed of when you first walked down the aisle. You can even embrace the principles that will make you satisfied in every walk of life!

I hope that you are blessed by this book. Getting blessed is important, but it is even more important that you become a blessing, that you become someone else's miracle. When you are casual, you eventually become a casualty. You are on earth for a purpose: to display God's glory through your relationships. Be deliberate and determined to receive the wholeness you need, and then purpose to help others to the same.

We have not because we ask not – we pray not. The power of God will be available for the harvest when we pray. Prayer releases personal holiness and hunger for God. It brings the power of God back into our world. The only reason we do not go forth in such power is that we ask not. Don't settle for anything less than God's infinite glory and presence demonstrated through your life and relationships. As you *read* this book, *pray* through this book. There's a miracle in your spouse!

Tommy Barnett
Pastor, Phoenix First Assembly

CONTENTS

A NEW POINT OF VIEW

The present states of your marriage relationship, your finances, your career and your health are what they are. But is that all there is? No! There is a fresh way of looking at life. There is a bright gleam of hope and a divine connection that invites the power of God's revelation to give you a new point of view, full of life and light and love. And suddenly, everything changes! Here's how our quest began…

***

It was the worst day of my life.

Never will I forget that moment when Bob stalked angrily out of the room without saying a word, leaving me alone with my tears, my shame, my guilt and my fear. I had just finished the hardest task I had ever had to do: confess to Bob, the love and joy of my life, that I had committed adultery. Now Bob was gone and I had no idea when, or if, he would return.

Alone with my thoughts, I wondered what would happen next. Fear rolled over me like a tidal surge as I realized that I stood on the brink of losing everything that was most precious to me: my husband, my children, my marriage, our ministry, the respect of my parents and our colleagues in ministry and, most of all, the sweet fellowship with God that I had known for so many years.

What had I done? The joy, happiness, excitement and contentment we had known – were they gone forever, destroyed beyond saving by my sinful and foolish act? Guilt and regret welled up in me to overflowing as I wept. In the midst of my tears I cried out desperately to God for help. Was there any hope? Marriages break up all the time over issues less serious than this. What chance did we have? Could anything ever be the same again? How I wished I could turn back the clock! We had been so happy…and now this. Was our marriage finished? Would we become another sad statistic in the divorce culture? More than anything in the world I wanted to reconcile with Bob. But was it possible? After what I had done, would Bob want to reconcile with me?

***

Shock. Utter, complete shock.

That was my first reaction when Audrey confessed her adultery to me. I sat there in stunned silence. Had I heard her correctly? Had she really said what I had thought I'd heard? How could the wife I had lived with and loved for nearly twenty years—and who I had thought loved me—be unfaithful to me? It was almost beyond belief. I simply could not take it in. This bombshell that had just blown our happy life to bits left me numb and speechless.

As the reality of Audrey's confession sank in, confusion quickly overtook my shock. I wanted to ask, "Audrey, did you really do this to me?" I longed to run away. But I didn't. Where would I go? I needed to leave her alone to clean up the mess and try to explain her betrayal. I just wanted out.

To tell you the honest truth, at that moment I didn't know what to do. The bottom had just fallen out of my life and I was scrambling for a foothold—any foothold. It was like trying to navigate unfamiliar terrain in the middle of the night with no light. I did not know what to do, but with all the powerful and potentially dangerous emotions welling up in me, I had to do something.

In the end I simply walked out without a word. I couldn't tell Audrey where I was going because I didn't know myself. Besides, at that moment I didn't know how to speak to her or be near her. Could we—would we—be reconciled? Could our marriage be saved? Did I even want it to be saved? At that point I did not know.

To Reconcile or Not to Reconcile

What do you do when your marriage is strained to the breaking point? How do you deal with the boiling cauldron of conflicting emotions stirred up by marital conflict? What do you do about disappointed expectations, broken dreams or continual disagreement over money matters or family priorities? What do you do when the worries and struggles of daily life have extinguished the flame of passion?

If infidelity is involved, how do you handle the hurt, the anger, the bitterness, the betrayal, the shattered trust? What do you do when you can't stand to be in the same room with the one you love because the pain of betrayal hurts too much?

If marital discord is driving you down, it's natural to assume that you have only two choices: You can fight or you can flee. You can dig in your heels and not yield an inch to the forces that are trying to destroy your relationship or you can throw up your hands in surrender and beat a hasty retreat. We would like to present you with a third option that introduces extreme hope and life-altering transformation.

A New Point of View

Since writing our first book, *Marriage Under Cover*, we have heard thousands of stories of painful circumstances as well as of newfound hope. Many times we cry, sometimes for joy as we read about victory, and sometimes in compassion as our hearts break for the painful circumstances that married couples are enduring. We used to wish we could give people something to help them through, a way to let them know there's still a future and a hope and, most of all, that they are loved. The good news is, we have found the perfect gift to give such a person, and we want to share it with you. It's simply this: a new point of view. It is often impossible to change our circumstances, but God has given each of us the ability and opportunity to choose the way we look at them.

Mark 10 gives the account of a beggar who found out that Jesus was passing by. How would Bartimaeus tell his story?

I Don't See Right

As I made my way near to the city entrance that warm summer day, the streets were abnormally quiet. The typical sounds of the venders selling their goods and the smells of fresh baked bread were missing. As I approached the corner to find a place in the shade I called out to my friends, "Where is everyone?"

Their friendly voices replied, "They're all on the other side of town."

Feeling a little puzzled but not alarmed, I found my usual place and sat down. Turning to my left to speak with Larry, who was lame, I continued with my questions. "There must be a reason everyone's over there. I mean, business is always better on this side of town. What could be the great attraction?" Asking Larry was better than your modern search engines; he knew everything about everything and everyone. Yet his answer was slow in coming. I could sense by the sound of his voice that he really didn't want to tell me. "Come on, Larry, ol' buddy, tell me," I said.

"Well, Bartimaeus, don't get up and run off when I tell you, but Jesus from Galilee is in town," he answered.

Oh, if you could have felt the excitement and anticipation that raced through my heart! You see, often my dad and I would stay up late at night talking about all the things we had heard throughout the day. Dad spent most of his time hanging out by the local temple. He loved to hear the Scriptures being read and would recite them for me at night. He had a great memory and was able to bring the Torah to life with his storytelling. He would talk about our forefathers, Abraham,

Isaac and Jacob; but he enjoyed the prophets the most. We would dream for hours about the promised Messiah and what it would be like to be free. I mean, really free! I don't mean to complain; Dad and I had a great life, but the Roman rule at times was oppressive. Still, they couldn't take the dream from our hearts.

For the past few years we had been hearing rumors about this great Teacher, Jesus the Nazarene, Who was being followed by large crowds eager to watch Him perform dynamic miracles. Some were claiming that He might be the Messiah! This made for great late night conversations with Dad as he recited all the passages that refer to this coming King.

His miracles fascinated me. I would sit at the corner all day with my friends, and the conversation almost became irritating to them at times as I would grow so excited at the possibility of one day having Jesus pass by. I could see it so clearly with my mind's eye. I knew exactly what I would do, and I would share these details with the gang. They were all happy to have someone in the group with a little optimism, but my good friend Larry never gave me much encouragement. In his matter of fact way he would bring everything down to a sobering reality: "Bartimaeus, you're blind. You and your father were both born blind; that's just the way it is. What do you want?"

I would quickly reply, "I want to see! One day, Larry, when Jesus passes by, no one's gonna keep me back; I'm going to Jesus!"

When I awoke that day I had no idea what awaited me—my own personal audience with Jesus! Although the streets were empty, I had hope. If Jesus was on His way to Jerusalem, He had to pass by me; it was only a matter of time. All I could do was wait. I chattered a blue streak on the corner that morning, knowing in my heart that Jesus would pass by. Larry tried to share my excitement, but his current reality wouldn't let him escape to dreams of a better life.

Soon we began to hear the crowd. I shouted for a play-by-play description because I wanted to know every detail. As the crowd drew near I began to shout again and again, "Jesus, Son of David, have mercy on me!" Voices from the crowd yelled back, telling me to be quiet.

Tears of desperation rolled down my cheeks. Then I felt a poke in my ribs. It was Larry.

He shouted at me, "Louder, Bartimaeus, shout louder!" I cupped my hands to my mouth and shouted, "Son of David, have mercy on me!"

Then, as though everything had gone silent and all those around me had disappeared, I heard a voice: "Tell him to come here."

Everything then jumped into fast motion. Larry began to shout with an excitement I had never heard from him before. "Cheer up, He's calling you!" I leapt to my feet, threw my beggar's cloak aside and began to pull my way through the crowd. I was going to Jesus!

As I stood before him I felt the touch of the back of His hand wiping my tears away. In a voice both gentle and strong, He asked, "What do you want Me to do for you?"

Without hesitation I fell to my knees. "Teacher," I said, "I want to see!"

Jesus replied, "Go your way. Your faith has healed you."

Instantly, I could see!

***

For the past several years this story has brought us great inspiration. For us it is more than the miracle of a blind man receiving his sight; it is faith being expressed as he receives his new point of view. Bartimaeus cries at the top of his lungs, "I want to see right! I can't see!" And Jesus gives him new sight. We are convinced that Jesus has extended an invitation to you. What do you want? Our prayer is that in your present circumstances you'll begin to tell the Lord, "I want to see." There are so many times we just don't see right. We need a new point of view.

A very significant part of this story is Bartimaeus's reply to the invitation to go to Jesus. As he leaps to his feet, he throws his cloak to the side. This is no ordinary cloak, but rather one that would have been given to him by the Roman government to signify that he was a genuine blind man deserving of alms. This cloak was Bartimaeus' source of income. For years it had been his identity. Every day before walking through the streets to find his place in the shade, he would put on this beggar's cloak. When he threw his beggar's cloak aside, he knew there would be no contingency plan. Determined in his heart never to return to a beggar's lifestyle again, he moved with confidence: "I'm going to Jesus." As a result, Bartimaeus received a new point of view.

So the question is, what cloak are you wearing? Are you allowing it to identify you? What is the first thing people see or perceive about you? For me, Bob, it was a victim mentality. My beautiful bride had betrayed me. All my dreams were gone. Our marriage was now tainted and I could only see life through the effects of adultery. But what I learned, and what I want to help you to lay hold of, is that Jesus is passing by! He wants to give you new sight, He wants to give you a new point of view.

On the other hand, for me, Audrey, it was the cloak of shame. Even though I knew and understood the Bible, it seemed virtually impossible for me to receive forgiveness for the sin of adultery. I mean, I knew better! Even though I had spent my entire life asking Jesus to forgive me of my sins and receiving that forgiveness, this was different. I didn't deserve forgiveness. My life was disqualified, discarded and tainted as a result of my extreme selfishness.

When I walked into a room full of fellow Christians, I felt the effects of shame. My sin was known; I was open to public humiliation and ridicule. I imagined all the glares from people with big black markers ready to write their X's on me, identifying me as the one who had sinned and betrayed her husband. I could read the message in the thick cloud that seemed to want to cover me: disqualified sinner.

At first I didn't understand how friends and acquaintances could be so offended by what I had done. My sin wasn't against them; it was against Bob! Why were they judging me so severely? Since then, and after years of healing, I believe I have a greater understanding of how we influence a much larger circle than our immediate family. I can now see how my sin was devastating to those whom I had influenced to follow Jesus. This didn't add up to them, and their disappointment even challenged their own faith as they tried to come to terms with my participation with sin. My heart is saddened that I have caused them grief.

As I've repented to the Lord for bringing disappointment not only to my own family but also to the family of God, I've asked Him to heal those who couldn't understand my sin and have struggled to forgive me. I experienced godly sorrow for the effects on others of the adultery in my life. But the story doesn't stop there.

Since I have owned all of this even more deeply, God has changed my point of view. I could never "make up" for my mistake; but as Jesus lives His life through me, He redeems the past. I received a radical new point of view to see myself the way Jesus sees me: robed in righteousness and wearing a crown of glory, with the oil of joy dripping off my robe so that the X's won't stick but will slip off. I have come into obedience to His point of view. The strength and authority that God has given me to be absolutely convinced that He does not hold my sin against me is contagious. Second Corinthians 5:7 says that He has called me to be an ambassador to proclaim that God is not holding my sin against me! God is not mad at me! His forgiveness is complete, and His cleansing is purifying. My heart aches for those who have held onto their shame, not receiving the amazing grace of Jesus to cover them! My heart celebrates for those who can hear the good news of this gospel message and be free!

What Cloak Are You Wearing?

You may be struggling with a variety of identities that the beggar's cloak represents: shame, hurt, disappointment, words people have spoken over you, worthlessness, fear of man, the ravages of sin. Are you willing to go to God's throne of grace and receive mercy and gain His point of view?

For this is the secret: Christ lives in you, and this is your assurance that you will share in his glory (Colossians 1:27b).

Christ in you is your confident expectation and hope that God's view and opinion of you, which is your glory, will become your reality.

That's the best news you'll ever hear in your life. May the magnitude of this truth be established in your heart.

I Am a Friend of God

Before embracing what it means to be best friends and best lovers with each other, let's explore what God has to say about friendship with us! We have found Romans chapter five to be extremely encouraging!

"Therefore, since we have been made right in God's sight by faith, we have peace with God because of what Jesus Christ our Lord has done for us. Because of our faith, Christ has brought us into this place of highest privilege where we now stand, and we confidently and joyfully look forward to sharing God's glory.

"We can rejoice, too, when we run into problems and trials, for we know that they are good for us – they help us learn to endure. And endurance develops strength of character in us, and character strengthens our confident expectation of salvation. And this expectation will not disappoint us. For we know how dearly God loves us, because he has given us the Holy Spirit to fill our hearts with his love.

"When we were utterly helpless, Christ came at just the right time and died for us sinners. Now, no one is likely to die for a good person, though someone might be willing to die for a person who is especially good. But God showed his great love for us by sending Christ to die for us while we were still sinners. And since we have been made right in God's sight by the blood of Christ, he will certainly save us from God's judgment. For since we were restored to friendship with God by the death of his Son while we were still his enemies, we will certainly be delivered from eternal punishment by his life. So now we can rejoice in our wonderful new relationship with God – all because of what our Lord Jesus Christ has done for us in making us friends of God" (Romans 5:1-11).

We've realized that we would be unable to eat, drink, breathe or live without our friendship with God, much less stay married as best friends and best lovers! What Jesus did for us in making us His friends is a gift too marvelous to comprehend, and we choose to receive and embrace it.

The richest people in the world are not those with the most money, but those with loving friends and lifelong relationships. Godly friendship is truly a priceless commodity. It's a gift of love and commitment that fulfills many of our deepest human needs.

Tapping into the resource of enjoying our spouse as our closest friend and expressing that love through intimacy gets us to the point of this book: becoming best friends and best lovers.

Bob's Turn

Audrey loves to describe her dreamy fantasy of what best friends are like: They are in constant communion, electrified conversation, spontaneous rendezvous...and did I mention a huge amount of talking? And not just surface talk, either. Best friends are constantly baring their hearts, speaking advice and wisdom and offering much comfort and consolation. But is this the kind of "best friends" that she wants us to be in our marriage? It sounds exhausting! I say all this with tongue in cheek, because fulfilling my ideal of a best lover would most likely exhaust her as well!

So where do we begin as husband and wife, each internalizing deep expectations and daring dreams that have calmed down to a slight fizzle, simply because the cares of life have thwarted success thus far? It all begins on the road of right relationship. As you travel with us here, look forward to a transformed heart and a changed life!

Your Friendship Together

We have written this book because we consider each other to be our very best friends. A phrase from the Song of Songs comes to mind: *"This is my beloved, and this is my friend"* (Song 5:16, KJV). The Bible rates friendship so highly that what passes for friendship in our day often pales by comparison. As we seek to have a biblical kind of relationship in our marriage, kindness and equality mark our friendship as we abandon positions, popularity and pedestals and simply give and receive.

Where husbands and wives are true friends, the conflict over headship and what that means in a marriage becomes meaningless. Who ever argues between friends as to who has the final say, or who is boss? It's this aspect of equality that makes God's choice of friendship with us so amazing. His kindness to us is an example and challenge as we pursue deep friendship within our marriage.

In the chapters that follow you will find eight characteristics of a satisfied heart that will help you become irresistible to your spouse. Once you discover that being best friends and best lovers encompasses enjoying spontaneous laughter, embracing secure commitment, enjoying sweet conversation, understanding selfless surrender, getting pleasure from satisfying sex, benefiting from screaming freedom, recognizing settled trust and anticipating soaring together, your relationship will never be the same!

You'll notice that we'll be looking at eight characteristics. The number eight represents new beginnings. Here you will encounter truths that will, if you allow them, penetrate your heart and rattle all the paradigms that have held you captive in a lifestyle and mindset of never having enough. These truths will equip you, should you so choose, to overcome all the "self stuff" that permeates our society and embrace the possibility of having it all...a satisfied heart. Jesus is passing by. Throw off the cloak and run to Him. A new point of view awaits you.

They Thought It Was Over...

At the end of a conference, one couple came forward to thank us for our ministry. They were going home together and couldn't wait to tell their young children that they would all live together again. They had been separated for a year and now, after learning about radical forgiveness for an entire weekend, they had renewed their covenant vows for each other and were excited about starting their married life together…again.

We asked them how they got there together. "Why a marriage conference? You're separated!" They giggled as they let us know what happened. Several weeks prior to the event, she had been listening to a local Christian radio station and had won tickets to the conference! She didn't want to attend alone, so she had told her estranged husband about it. He agreed to go, and the rest is history!

Glossary of Terms

Best Friends:

They share everything. Their strong foundation holds them strong through adversity and ecstasy. They are comfortable either in each other's silence or in electrifying conversation. They laugh together, dream together, cry together and pray together. Nothing can drive them apart from each other, for they know they are deeply loved, and that is never questioned.

Best Lovers:

They have privileges that no other human being will have. They know each other's intricate parts and can give freely and unashamed. Whether it's a gentle touch or a wave of passion, their expression of love is always unselfish. And no one will ever know what they have shared, for it is between two only.

The Number Eight:

The number eight represents new beginnings. The past will not dictate the future, nor will it hinder the dreams that refuse to die. Faith is ignited and the fear of the future is dissipated. God's mercy is new every single morning.

Satisfied:

Content and full of joy. Ready to give out of overflow. Completely protected, provided for and loved. Not selfish, jealous or needy for more, those who are satisfied exude perfect peace, thankfulness and God's heavenly presence.

Heart:

Your innermost being and the dwelling place of God. The deep inner sanctuary where decisions are made, desires are formed and motives are created. The most holy place of your being, your very core.

1

SPONTANEOUS LAUGHTER

We love laughing. Healthy laughter is an expression of delight and joy, and it springs from a sense of well-being and peace. If you're struggling with serious unhappiness in your marriage, let us encourage you: Your best days are ahead! You can learn to rise above present circumstances and begin dreaming and laughing together! That's what being best friends and best lovers is all about! Let's face it, we live in a world where busy-ness, responsibility and the cares of the world can be overwhelming. Releasing laughter is one of the keys to being satisfied in love. At the same time, laughter will decrease stress and unlock healing for your body, mind and spirit.

There are going to be challenges in your marriage, and seasons of serious scenarios. It's not exactly easy to laugh when your heart is filled with depression, anger, resentment, bitterness or fear. Our dear friend, Dr. Don Colbert, says, "Laughter is as powerful as a drug, very inexpensive and has absolutely no side effects, except for the proverbial bursting your sides from laughing so hard."[1] *"A cheerful heart is good medicine, but a broken spirit saps a person's strength"* (Proverbs 17:22).

Jesus spoke of the childlike trust in the Father that expresses freedom, joy and delight (Matthew 18:2-4). Children laugh quickly and easily, for in most cases they are free from the stress and baggage that hinders laughter and steals joy. When we smile at each other we affect each other's spirit; smiling is contagious! We encourage our children to smile at people—often! It's amazing to see how many times the smile is returned.

Our prayer as you hold this book is that you will find joy that rises above circumstances and focuses on the very character of God. We're convinced that when He becomes the grandest, most influential, most powerful source of joy in life, any other relationship will pale in determining your mood, your attitudes and your outlook. Every one of us has

> *The quest for love and happiness is a natural human drive. And believe it or not, it's what God wants for you, too!*

access to Him to the degree that we will receive Him and everything He has promised. The psalmist described his security in God: *"You will show me the way of life, granting me the joy of your presence and the pleasures of living with you forever"* (Psalm 16:11). When your heart is healed, content, joyful and satisfied, laughter comes quickly, easily and often. The first key to becoming satisfied is found within your heart.

A Satisfied Heart

This book is all about you and about your finding satisfaction in love and life. Be honest, now; isn't that what you really want? Everybody does. The quest for love and happiness is a natural human drive. And believe it or not, it's what God wants for you, too! Sit back for a moment and allow your dreams to be awakened. Try to imagine how it would feel to be completely, extravagantly and outrageously satisfied. Does this sound selfish? Surprisingly, the exact opposite is true.

A satisfied heart is one that is at rest, for it lacks nothing! A satisfied heart gives without measure, simply because it has received so much. A satisfied heart is generous because fulfillment and contentment banish all selfishness.

You are exceptional, purposeful and irresistible. You may not believe these things about yourself, but the treasures of your true identity and your intrinsic value are hidden in the depths of your heart. You will discover them when your heart is satisfied in God, for it is then that you will be able to cease from struggling and striving and know your place of rest and peace. You're living on a gold mine; there is abundance! The search is on!

Your heart represents your innermost being – the dwelling place of God and your inner sanctuary. It is the very depth of your being where your desires and passions meet your will and motivation. The heart is where all that really affects your life takes place. Most importantly, this is where you converse with Almighty God. We want to journey to this most holy place and debunk the theory that this is too difficult to understand or is only for the elite. God has chosen to make you His dwelling place. He invites you to have a moment-by-moment interactive relationship with Him.

We find that most people in this world are dissatisfied. They're struggling with disappointment, a sense of lack and a restless desire for something more. The squeeze is on! The outside pressures of life are like a vice. Every day that vice is turned tighter and tighter until such people are ready to burst. Most people live from their minds and emotions and never live from their hearts. The life source of such people is extremely limited and shallow. We want to connect you to your heart. We want to take you to where you can commune with God so that when the pressures of life come in you can remain unchanged. We have found the source of life in the Holy Spirit that releases the light, life and love of God's character. Your heart is where the real you resides and where the true condition of your spirit is revealed.

You have probably heard it said, *"Out of the overflow of the heart the mouth speaks"* (Matthew 12:34, NIV). Eventually, whatever is in your heart will come out in your speech. So if you've ever heard things come out of your mouth that were less than admirable, you are, like all the rest of us, a candidate for spiritual heart surgery. This is the first step in becoming best friends and best lovers with your spouse and to having a satisfied heart!

There are plenty of self-help products around that promise to give you practical ways to change your behavior and enjoy a great life and successful relationships. They require a lot of self-implementation and will work, but they are all about behavior modification. As long as you work the system you feel pretty good! You begin to gain a great amount of identity and success and fulfillment from your accomplishments! Unfortunately, these methods work only as long as you discipline yourself to perform and to remember the to-do list! What's exalted and put on the pedestal is self – the same self that comes crashing down when you forget to perform! You become self-judging because you have wrapped your identity and worth in what you have been able to accomplish.

But don't despair! There is a finished work for you that will cause you to know your true identity and your place of rest. You can be satisfied, no matter what your external circumstances say.

What would happen if we stopped concentrating on changing our behavior and instead began to pursue a transformed heart? That would be getting to the very root of the issue. The core of our problem as human beings is that we need an entirely new start.

Instead of taking your old heart – the one that is wounded, probably broken several times and full of pain, shame, guilt, bitterness and regret – instead of trying to mend it and make it better yourself, imagine what God can do for you. He promises to give you a brand new heart, one that has new desires and a new nature. God can transform you radically from the inside out until what used to take work and discipline suddenly becomes effortless and natural. That is heart transformation as opposed to behavior modification.

The easiest way to discover your heart condition is through simple observation: How thankful are you on a daily basis? Can you look beyond your present unhappy circumstances and still be thankful for God's love and blessings? All of us have something to be thankful for, even in the midst of extreme pain and external pressures. Satisfaction in life is not an external condition based on possessing everything you've ever dreamed of and being continually surrounded by peace, love and joy in every relationship. Satisfaction is a heart condition that rises above circumstances and finds joy even in times of suffering. It is learning, like Paul, to be content in whatever situation you find yourself because you are secure in the love and grace of God (see Philippians 4:11).

As parents of four children, we know a little bit about someone wanting something! Those times when all of the Meisners are overflowing with thankfulness and contentment at the same time are like kisses from heaven! No begging for more, no complaints, no comparisons. In the same way, we imagine our heavenly Father loves to know that we are satisfied with His goodness and unfailing love actually pursuing us all the days of our lives! We don't know about you, but we want to live all of our days in His house, including our days right here and right now! We want heaven on earth—and we want it in our marriage too!

Why, you might ask, do we begin a book about best friends and best lovers talking about a satisfied heart? The reason is simple: A satisfied heart has much to give. And you can't give away what you don't have. If you are not extravagantly loved, how can you give extravagant love to another? If you do not value yourself, how will you be able to value your spouse? So you see, this really is all about you. And it's definitely all about your heart.

I'm Not Satisfied

When your heart is not satisfied you will exude selfishness and neediness. We have all met people like this, people crying out for someone to fill the vacant gap in the crevices of their broken hearts. An unsatisfied heart senses lack, resulting in a craving that demands to be filled. And apart from a satisfying love relationship with the Lord, our sinful selfish nature will quickly seek other, often deadly remedies: the sins of the flesh.

Christ has called us to a life of freedom; not the freedom to satisfy our sinful nature, but freedom to serve one another in love. Our old sinful nature loves to do evil, which is the opposite of the desire of the Holy Spirit. But the Spirit plants new desires in our hearts that are the opposite of those of the sinful nature. These two forces are constantly fighting each other. Our choices are never free from this conflict.

We are all selfish by nature; we were born that way! Unfortunately, we will never be immune from selfishness as long as we live on this earth. Many folks spend their lives indulging their sinful natures until they reach rock bottom, where they finally give their lives to God and realize their need for forgiveness.

**

My (Audrey's) experience was just the opposite of this. The most selfish moment in my life did not come when I had reached the bottom, but rather when I was on top. I had it all! My husband loved me and I loved him. We thoroughly enjoyed our three children. I had a thriving career hosting a secular morning show that made me well known in my sphere of influence. I was at my ideal weight and I had a weekly house-cleaning service. Bob worked for my parents in their television ministry. We both loved helping people. In addition to our other activities we had started a church and were pioneering a tremendous work of God in our city. What more could a Jesus girl want?

Then a young man we were assisting started to pay a lot of attention to me. He was highly complimentary and loved being friends with me. Believing I was invulnerable to any kind of impure relationship, I let myself enjoy his attention. Gradually, almost without realizing it, my heart became dissatisfied with what I had. My selfish nature kicked in and I found myself wanting more. I wanted him, too! That's the way sin is. It is never, ever satisfied. What at first seem like small compromises soon lead to big compromises and a major downward shift in attitude and moral sensitivity. Such compromises are always dangerous. In my case, they led to adultery.

Perhaps now you can understand our passion for you and your

spouse to have hearts that are truly satisfied. We want to protect you from the pain that we experienced, as well as provide tools to help you achieve and maintain complete satisfaction in God and in each other.

After I committed adultery, I came to my senses with a sudden shock of horror at what I had done. I quickly confessed my sin to Bob which was the hardest thing I have ever had to do. That's when the pain and horror of my betrayal really began to torture us! Adding to our anguish was the discovery that I was pregnant as a result of the affair.

Do you see where my unsatisfied heart took me? My world suddenly changed radically. I was pregnant, suicidal, forced to move to a new city with no friends, no career, no ministry and very little money. And there definitely was no house-cleaning service! My reputation was certain to be ripped from underneath me because this baby would look different from my other children. The worst part was that I now had a husband who was struggling with knowing how to relate to me. Fear was my constant companion, especially the fear that our precious children would be scarred and wounded, and our marriage would never be the same because of my selfish and stupid act.

***

How do we combat our sinful, selfish nature? In our own power we cannot. As much as selfishness is natural, God's extravagant, perfect love is supernatural. And it's the power of His love that covers our sins, transforms our hearts and satisfies us to the fullest. The only way to counteract selfishness is with the opposite force of satisfaction – the complete contentment that comes only from being connected to the supernatural Source of life and love and all other things.

Being satisfied means that you have no hunger for lustful pleasure because your "pleasure-meter" is full of good things! Being satisfied means that you are not jealous of what other people have or even of who they are because you know exactly who you are, and your identity in your heavenly Father is secure. Being satisfied means that you don't have outbursts of anger because you are at peace and not relying on those around you to fulfill certain expectations. Being satisfied means that you know true pleasure – godly pleasure.

This journey is all about you and really has very little to do with your spouse. But read on, for there is much hope here for your marriage. Your dreams must be ignited as you imagine what married life would be like if you and your spouse were best friends and best lovers. Our own journey of restoration took us to tortuous valleys of pain, yet we are on the other side now, calling and pleading for others to join us as we enjoy a marriage even better and deeper than it has ever been before. Become satisfied in love and reap the rewards. Forge ahead!

**

What Do I Actually Do?

I, Audrey, encountered a distinct milestone for my own heart over a period of seven days. It was an extremely unusual time for me. It was Easter week, a time of year when I have always been surrounded by family, food, tradition and a full schedule! This particular year, however, was completely different. For various reasons, every person who is closest to me had to leave town. Bob left with my parents on a trip to Israel. Our eldest son was attending Bible school in Dallas, Texas. Our daughter was away with her cousin, and our middle son went away to be with friends.

For seven whole days I was left with a completely empty schedule and with no family around. No one, that is, except Robert, our youngest son, who was three years old at the time. This was not planned; it just seemed to happen. And while this may not sound unusual to some, it was very strange for me. I have not had time alone without significant others for more than an afternoon in my whole life; my calendar had not been that empty for years. I had no responsibilities at work and no expectations from anyone for an entire seven days. When unusual circumstances come upon you, it's a good time to ask some strategic questions. What in the world should I do with all this time?

As the time grew closer, I began to make plans and preparation. Instead of calling every friend I knew and trying to fill some time with social activity, I did the opposite. I decided that I would not answer the phone or turn on the TV, but would deliberately turn up the truth in my heart and ask God for a renewal in my spirit and for transformation.

In this season of my life I was asking tough questions and I wanted direct answers. I communicated my desires to the Lord and asked Him for direction in order to make my time alone most valuable and effective. As though I were planning for heart surgery, I entered into this time cleansed from the past and, anticipating a remedy for my desperate heart, I acquired tools for the task. I was willing to be transformed, regardless of the cost.

What transpired during those seven days changed my life forever. Heart transformation took place. I learned that in order to effectively allow God to transform my heart I had to write His truth on my heart. In order to gain access to my heart to write His truth there, I had to first get through my mind, thoughts and intellect, for my mind was the gatekeeper to my heart. Learning to rest my mind and body helped me to access my heart. It was in very still, quiet moments with the Lord that I meditated on His Word, His truth and His opinions and character.

Very simple and profound truths replaced the lies that I had believed and that had formed destructive patterns in my thoughts and behavior. Lies the enemy had whispered had t be rooted out, lies such as, "I have to fear lack, because I never have enough finances." Deception has nothing to do with truth, yet it presents itself as truth; but it is rooted in lies. I knew God wanted to give me the desires of my heart, but I also knew I didn't deserve them; therefore I would always be in want! Another whisper: "I'll never be secure in the future because I need to be more successful. And if I want to be more successful, I must find ways to promote myself and strategically make a way for myself."

God engraved His truth in the very heart of who I am, right where I commune with Him. I never have to worry or be afraid of the future, for my Father in heaven will not leave me — ever. He will always provide for me. Not only does He promise this, but He has also has brought me to the place of highest privilege, calling me His very daughter. I do not have to work hard and be smart to promote myself, for I am at rest in Him. No good thing will He withhold from me. He has given me desires that He wants to fulfill because of His extreme love for me!

During that time His truth became my reality. I stopped questioning. Every day of those seven days, several times a day, I took time to write the truth on my heart. Christ actually lives His life through me; it is no longer I who live! In Christ, we have the opportunity to experience the great exchange: our life for His, and His realities! It is His opinion; therefore it is His reality…including the thousands of promises He has made to mankind. We don't experience these promises because we beg God; we experience them when they become part of our reality! When we accept His view and opinion as our own, we become infused with that reality.

I faced a question: Would I surrender my view and opinion and accept God's views and opinions? God desires our surrender as a way to lift us up, not to humiliate us. His view and opinion are much higher than our own. So, I am who He says I am. I can do what He says I can do. I have all that He says I have. My reality changes as I embrace His truth, for heart beliefs stimulate actions that require no conscious effort. Everything God has for us is within our reach.

Most of my behavior was a product of how I saw myself. The way I saw myself caused me to function in effortless motion. My behavior took place without thought or conscious intention. As I put my efforts into one place I experienced the power of being, for God is a heart God. Transformation took place as I renewed my mind – the way I saw myself – and got connected to Jesus, where I started "being." And the "doing" took care of itself!

In a practical sense, adding and taking away takes constant effort. When we're always trying to do better, we enter into an internal conflict. For example, we want to begin being more patient with our spouse. We set a goal to be a better, more patient and kind person. We add patience and peace to our life and subtract pride and impatience. But when I have God's promise that I am loved hidden in my heart and I don't have to live up to my own expectations of efficiency or the fear of failing, then I am introduced to the power of transformation! The vicious circle of trying hard to change finally gives way to a journey of truth with a transformed heart.

It was after this heart transformation took place that I walked in a new sense of peace in my heart. And it was my new point of view, an exchange of my thoughts for His thoughts about pain and pleasure, that sealed the victory!

***

Pain and Pleasure

It is human nature to gravitate toward pleasure and resist pain. But when it comes to choosing what causes pain and pleasure, there's a lot of confusion floating around.

Most people grow up with a paradigm about pain and pleasure that could not be further from the truth. In a nutshell, it is this: I need to make good choices. So, I choose to live for God. It's painful. I have to give up the pleasures that make the world fun. I'll be a martyr and sacrifice. It's my duty. At least I'll be the one going to heaven one day! The sinners had their fun for a while, but they'll be sorry!

So this person goes about making the hard, yet better, choices. Temptation comes their way and their "pleasure-antennas" are alerted. Oh, that would feel so good! Maybe I'll just do it once. It's so enticing, so seducing, so satisfying! After several compromises, their guilty conscience kicks in and they kick themselves and turn back to the Lord. They face their walk of pain once again. Until the next promise of pleasure passes by!

The enemy of our soul loves this easy trap! Because of his lies to us about God's true character and his persuasive ideas that there's more somewhere else or that we will be more fulfilled if we go his way, we end up equating pleasure with sin. In reality, sin always leads to death. Every time! Death, destruction, turmoil, torture, loss, confusion, darkness and eternal loneliness. The pleasure of sin lasts only for a short season!

Choosing God's way is choosing eternal promises for abundance, provision, protection, love, peace and joy unspeakable – as well as intense freedom! What more could one want? God is pleasure person-ified, and His life in us brings complete satisfaction.

Selfishness is the powerful beast that tempts us to sin and feeds our deep destructive cravings. Unfortunately, selfishness is a natural part of our fallen nature. But it is completely unnatural from the way God cre-ated us. It is selfishness that breeds the fruit of the selfish nature. Our new nature in Christ wars constantly with our old nature of sin, and we decide which one wins by which one we listen to. Only in the life to come will we be free of this conflict. And won't that be glorious!

The Constant Fight

So how do we combat that which is only natural? Only God's super-natural, infinite and perfect love can overcome our sinful nature, trans-form our hearts and bring deep and complete satisfaction. If we don't want to be selfish, then what's the opposite or opposing force that will counteract this self-serving, sin-motivating trait? It's being satisfied: completely content, fully convinced and connected to the source.

The satisfied life is a life lived to please the Spirit. Its harvest is everlasting life. This is a life that enables us to share another's troubles and problems and to help those in need. The satisfied person enjoys the personal satisfaction of having done work well and has no need to com-pare himself or herself to anyone else. Sound like a good life? It's avail-able to you right now!

Satisfy us in the morning with your unfailing love, that we may sing for joy and be glad all our days.

Psalm 90:14, NIV

A person who is whole and complete in Christ has an irresistible trait that exudes the kind of confidence that attracts others. You've probably heard the romantic phrase in a movie or a song: "You complete me." If that truly is the case in any relationship, trouble is already lurking at the door. If you are not complete and fully satisfied in God's love for you, if you don't have Jesus as your total Source to make you complete, you become needy.

While this attribute may seem attractive to one for a short season, "needy" simply doesn't cut it when it comes to being irresistible! Imagine the electricity, strength and passion when two complete people come together! That's the kind of relationship that will keep the spark of intimacy for the long run. That's the kind of relationship that grows in passion and encompasses best friends and best lovers.

Why Aren't We Laughing?

Cultivating a life of contentment, appreciation, forgiveness, joy, love and compassion is the perfect breeding ground for lots of spontaneous laughter. Once you understand that pleasure is associated with God, you will want to further this relationship! It's important to know that sin will always separate you from God, because He is holy. Getting a real understanding of sin has helped to protect us from so much pain. And it's hard to laugh when you're in pain!

There are some aspects of sin that should be clear in your heart. Sin is never, ever satisfied. It will always want more. Sexual sin will always become more and more perverted. Greed will never have enough. Pride will never absorb enough power. When sin is involved in any relationship there will be abuse, lies, betrayal and destruction. Sin is nothing but a painful and deadly trap.

Do you know what pure pleasure is? It's having intimacy with God and being complete in Him, satisfied and generously giving of this abundant life to others!

Sin is always dangerous. In chemistry class we learn that water, or H_2O, changes its state according to its environment. In its invisible form, it is steam. You hardly notice it's there. When cooled, it turns to liquid. It becomes noticeable and usable. At even colder temperatures it freezes and becomes hard. It can even become very sharp and solid enough to deal a death blow if strategically used. But it's all good old H_2O; there are just different forms caused by circumstantial change.

> ❄
> *We must deal with our thoughts, imaginations and dreams that are based on sin from the very beginning in order to be protected from the schemes of the enemy.*

It's exactly the same with sin. When sin is "just" a thought, it seems innocent. We think it's not going to hurt anyone; no one even needs to know about it. It's no big deal. Wrong! Any form of sin, from its first inception to full-blown participation, is sin from the start. We must deal with our thoughts, imaginations and dreams that are based on sin from the very beginning in order to be protected from the schemes of the enemy.

***

After participating in the sin of adultery, I saw the effect of the destruction, turmoil and torment it left in its wake. Yet the selfishness in me still wanted to enjoy the memories because my heart had not yet been changed. I asked Jesus to please let me see sin the way He sees it. I didn't want to try to stop thinking of it as pleasure; I wanted effortless victory! I wanted to know within the depths of my being that sin is something I hate and that I do not participate in because it will bring me pain! It may seem pleasurable for a season, but it always trails down the road to destruction, devastation and death.

As the exact opposite, death to self can be painful for a season, but the eternal pleasures will last forever, and a satisfied heart will be your reward.

The Lord brought me to places of deeper and deeper repentance until finally I saw my sin for what it really was. Now I have no desire at all to see that other man again. I don't find myself wondering what he's doing or how he's doing. I don't fantasize about being with him or cherish any memories with him as being happy. Today the very thought of that season of sin disgusts me!

Life will bring seasons of pain. No one is exempt! In fact it's during those times that great opportunities come to let the Lord go deep into your heart. As I look back at my times of pain during the healing process I can smile, knowing that God used those moments to minister peace, healing and wholeness to the depths of my heart. Don't waste those times; simply ask God to work that pain through you. Where you've experienced the greatest pain is where you'll have the greatest passion. It may take time, but as you let God heal you, you will long to help others in these same circumstances.

I am amazed how many marriages have been healed and restored as a direct result of our marriage testimony. That pain was not wasted, and now thousands are being helped. We have passion to boldly proclaim that no marriage is too messed up for God to come in and bring beauty and redemption.

***

God did not design marriage to complete you or to make you happy. He loves you enough to know that you need a partner in life to call you higher and to help you to deal with your own heart. It is during the painful times in life that we have the opportunity to write on our heart more than ever. Pain will drive us to become either bitter or better. When we cry out to God in pain and tell Him of our need for Him, we take Him into the deep places of our heart so He can give us truth and wisdom. It's usually the turbulent seasons in life that are the most monumental in terms of spiritual growth and defined character.

Our story has a parallel in the account of Hosea in the Bible. Hosea must have been astonished when God instructed him to forgive his wife Gomer. Long before, she had deserted him for a life of prostitution; she had returned to him only because time had rendered her undesirable and destitute. How could God ask Hosea to take back such a treacherous woman?

God was revealing something so intimate about Himself that Hosea could only understand if he could somehow experience what God was feeling. God wants us to understand how He feels about sin. It breaks His heart when one of His children is torn apart because of sin. If we let Him, God can and will break our hearts with the things that break His heart. His desire is not to hurt us, but to lead us into a more intimate relationship with Him. The amazing thing is that no matter how far we've strayed, God is willing to forgive us and welcome us back into His family.

***

When You Enjoy Life, the Laughter Comes Easily

Our culture glorifies the rich and famous, and so often we dream of being like them and having what they have. But a warped point of view will cause us to become bored over time with even the richest and best of luxuries. The most beautiful things in this world are free and are available to those who will seek them and take notice. When I, Audrey, stop noticing the beauty in nature around me, or the tenderness of a hug from one of my children, I need a new point of view. When Bob becomes irritating to me instead of irresistible, I need a new point of view.

One of my greatest personal challenges in life is impatience, especially when I get too busy and the deadlines are screaming. I suddenly lose tolerance for people around me, wondering why they are not as efficient as I am. And Bob usually receives the brunt of it. This is not the way to maintain a flourishing friendship! Bob quickly figures out that he's a disappointment to me, and who wants to hang around with someone who's disappointed in them? When this happens, my busy deadlines are now coupled with a bad mood but masked with a fake smile. My heart is not satisfied and I'm running around sporting an attitude that says, "Fine! I'll just do it myself!"

A satisfied heart enjoys life, even when circumstances are crazy. How clearly I remember the Sunday in church when an elderly gentleman from the United Kingdom was the guest speaker. At one point he stretched out his long, thin, bony finger at us and declared, "Beware of the baroness of Busy-ness." Many couples – perhaps you're one of them – are not enjoying the benefits of being best friends and best lovers, not because they don't want to, but because they are just too busy.

I can go through months at a time when, if I don't wake up with a list in my head and work steadily for fifteen hours, I will not accomplish what needs to get done for the day. I rarely sit down; when I do, it takes a conscious effort to relax. I'm telling you this because I know that most of you reading this have similar lives. Since I value relationships, I am always sure to prioritize and include relationships on my tasks list. I add items such as, "take time to play with my four-year-old"; "sit down with my seventeen-year-old today"; "look into Bob's eyes and tell him I love him." But what happens? Instead of being relationship-motivated, I become task-driven, even in my relationships!

Relationships can only go so far on task-driven gas. The fuel runs out and the energy ebbs away because duty, rather than passion, is the fuel. And all of a sudden the spontaneity is gone, along with the joy, fun and laughter. All that is left of the relationship is a vacant, empty shell.

On the opposite end of the spectrum, when you are living out of a heart full of peace and contentment, even the tasks that used to be a duty become a joy! It all depends on your point of view. Even family vacations can be spent on task because it's something you should do. Birthday parties and dinners become stress points instead of being some of the pleasures in life. If you are too busy to have fun in life, you are too busy. God created us with the capacity for pleasure and placed us in a world full of wonders to enjoy. Your capacity for joy, laughter and pleasure in any activity depends on the condition of your heart. It depends on your point of view.

I can go on a business trip and be in task mode: making lists, being serious and responsible, determined to get things done. Or, I can go on the same business trip with the same schedule and think differently. I can still get things done, but at the same time enjoy the pleasure of visiting new places, meeting new people and seeing the fruit of my labor.

Many are the times I have lived out of a place of duty for months on end, where even those things that should be pleasures become duties. Now, however, I am learning more and more to live out of a satisfied heart, so that even my duties become pleasures and laughter comes easily!

***

In duty mode, you can fake right behavior for only so long. When you truly enjoy something, however, it inspires passion and energy not only in you, but also in those who are around you. Passionate people are the ones who make an impact in this world. If you are passionate about life, people will know immediately where your heart is.

A doctor who enjoys promoting healing will inspire wellness in his patients.

A teacher who enjoys teaching will instill in her students a passion for learning.

A wife who enjoys being a wife will have a husband who is proud to call her his wife.

A parent who enjoys being a parent will raise confident, secure kids who know they are loved.

When the stresses of life take over, not only do your spouse and children play second fiddle to the furious frenzy, but your heart also suffers neglect. And your heart condition is of absolute importance at all times, for from it springs the way in which you live your life. We want you to enjoy being married and to experience restored laughter in your relationship! Enjoy being a husband! Enjoy being a wife! Take a deep breath and find something to laugh about!

Heart Revelation: The Tough Questions

What are the areas in which I am dissatisfied? Disappointed? Have a sense of lack? A restless desire for something more?

Am I committed to spiritual heart surgery, looking for a new heart with new desires?

Do I find my identity and worth in my accomplishments?

Do I look beyond my present unhappy circumstances and remain thankful for God's love and blessings?

Do I exhibit selfishness and neediness in my relationship?

Will I surrender my view and opinion and accept God's views and opinions of me?

What sin do I love the most? Am I willing to accept God's point of view, that this will result in pain?

Is my thought life safe right now? Or am I justifying "little" sinful thoughts?

Am I willing to use my pain as an opportunity for God to minister and to change my heart?

Am I too busy to pay attention to the most important things in life?

Heart Transformation: The Truth Established

Our best days are ahead. My hope and future is based on God's promises! (See Jeremiah 29:11.)

As I focus on God's character – His faithfulness, love, justice, mercy, goodness, holiness, forgiveness and grace – I can laugh in the face of adversity. (See Philippians 4:8.)

I have access to the Father and all of His promises are yes in Christ Jesus. I can rise above my circumstances! (See Galatians 3:21-22.)

As I rest in God and find my satisfaction in Him, I will lack no good thing. (See Psalm 84:11.)

It is the power of God's love that covers our sins, transforms our hearts and satisfies us to the fullest. (See Psalm 103.)

I never have to worry or be afraid of the future, for my Father in heaven will not leave me, ever. (See Hebrews 13:5-6.)

I will always be provided for because not only does my Father in heaven promise this, but He has brought me to the place of highest privilege, calling me His very own. (See Romans 5:2.)

I do not have to work hard and be quick to promote myself, for I am at peace in Him. (See Isaiah 26:3.)

No longer do I live, but Christ lives His life in me! (See Galatians 2:20.)

Transformation takes place as I renew my mind – the way I see myself – and get connected to Jesus, where I start "being." And the "doing" takes care of itself! (See Ephesians 5:25-27.)

True pleasure and outrageous joy are offshoots of living my life in Christ. (See Psalm 118:15.)

Where I have experienced pain is where I have the greatest passion. (Psalm 42:5-6.)

Prayer

Father in heaven, instead of taking my old heart, one that is wounded, probably broken several times and full of pain, shame, guilt, bitterness and regret, I thank You for Your promise to give me a brand new heart, one that has new desires and a new nature.

I choose Your eternal promises for abundance, provision, protection, love, peace, joy unspeakable and intense freedom! Thank You, God, that You are pleasure personified, and that experiencing Your life will give me complete satisfaction. I recognize my selfishness that tempts me to sin and feeds my deep destructive cravings. Father, forgive me. I don't want anything to do with sin. Cleanse me completely!

God, I need You. I'm asking for truth and wisdom. Please help me to grow spiritually as You define my character. You designed me for pleasure; I pray that I will enjoy life and laugh easily and often.

Spontaneous Laughter: It Was as though She Were Dead

We sat in a small room facing a young couple, and we knew there was trouble. Their faces told the story, and their words confirmed it. They had only been married two years. Confusion and unmet expectations had led to disaster in their relationship. He was in mourning, totally at a loss as to what to do. Her face was almost gray, she was numb to any emotion and she wanted out of the marriage. She watched her husband cry and she had no response. She had already begun another relationship with an abusive drug dealer.

Bob and the hurting husband left the room, and the young wife said to me, "I don't know who I am. I do not want to be here." I was at a complete loss; she wasn't responding to anything I said. However, as soon as I closed my eyes to pray, I instantly saw a vision in my heart of this same young woman worshipping Jesus! I was shocked, and said out loud, "You are a Jesus girl! You are a daughter of the King! You love to dance and worship!" As I opened my eyes I saw a tear roll down her face. In a monotone voice she said, "When worship was about to end, I used to beg God, 'Just ten more minutes in Your presence!' "

One tear turned into a cry from her heart. I had the privilege of ushering her into the arms of her Father in heaven who held her as she wailed and wept. She was lost, desolate and on the road to death – and Jesus healed her heart! What happened next astounded me. Joy began to spill over from this once lifeless human. Her eyes began to twinkle and her face was radiant with God's glory.

After we were finished praying, she ran out of the room, literally laughing and ran straight to her husband! She didn't just hug him; she jumped him! She wrapped her legs around his waist and squeezed him, and they began to twirl. Laughter was restored! The healing had begun, and it all started in the deep places of her heart.

---

[1]Don Colbert, MD, *Stress Less* (Siloam Press, 2005): 235.

2

SECURE COMMITMENT: THE DAY WE SAID "I DO"

When we wed, we got married for life. We dreamed of being together for a lifetime and felt like the whole world was ahead of us. The possibilities for love and life seemed endless. In this commitment of saying "yes" to each other, we also said "no" to everyone else.

Young and in love as we were, marriage fulfilled a dream and a goal for both of us. Before we married we deliberately made a decision never to mention the word "divorce." Divorce would never be an option, and that was clear in both of our hearts. If anyone had asked us how we felt so secure in getting married at such a young age, our answer would have been, "Our love is secure and strong. We know it's a lifetime love." As best friends with self-sacrificing companionship, we knew this was about more than just each of us individually.

We were two people becoming one.

Our marriage ceremony invited the presence of God. This was not just a union of two, but of Three. In front of a gathering of human witnesses we pledged ourselves before God and invited Him to be the very center point of our lives. We wanted our ceremony to be as symbolic as possible. We exchanged vows, rings, communion, and asked our parents and pastors to declare a blessing over our lives. The white gown representing the purity of the bride was there with purpose. We did everything that was traditional to our Western culture, and then some! One of our friends brought a banner down the aisle proclaiming, "As the bridegroom rejoices over the bride, so I rejoice over you."

We knew exactly what we were doing. There were no contingency plans. This was it forever, and we were both ecstatic to do this. We brought everything to the altar. Everything we had, every part of who we were, we laid down to start our life together. That is the amazing, powerful thing about a wedding ceremony. The day before, we were not married! Prior to that ceremony what was Bob's was Bob's and what was Audrey's was Audrey's. Then…we arrived at the church and proceeded through this beautiful, elaborate ceremony, exchanging words, prayers and songs. Finally, someone declared that by the power of the government we were Robert and Audrey Meisner!

In a moment everything changed. We now had rights, privileges and responsibilities. If we had slept together the night before our ceremony, that would have been wrong. The next night…wow! Isn't this great! What's the difference? It isn't that sex in itself is right or wrong; it's just that we were acknowledging God by participating in His design for having a right, healthy and whole marriage.

On our wedding day we gave each other equal access and right to our time, money, enjoyment, sexual intimacy, adequate family time, admiration – even our very being. Absolutely everything we owned. It was huge! That day we took on a new identity. No longer could you describe us apart from each other. We were one.

Finally, we made ourselves completely vulnerable to each other. We chose to honor each other. That meant we wouldn't shame, manipulate, criticize or withhold affection from one another. Ultimately, we realized it would be impossible to keep these commitments all the time without fail; but we also knew that when one of us did fail, the other wouldn't lash back and use the same tactic. We knew that we would not fight against each other, but would fight for our union. No longer were we going through life alone. We now had each other. We dreamed of growing old together, of seeing not only our children but also our grandchildren. In that, we saw great strength. We knew that we were better together than apart.

Preparation for marriage was something neither of us took lightly. Knowing it was a goal for both of us, we purposefully prepared ourselves in eager anticipation of that great day when we would be wed! We wanted our marriage to be exceptional; we wanted God to be glorified in everything we did. There are no two people on the earth exactly like us. Through this mystical union, we believed we would somehow fulfill a destiny designed in the heart of God and a purpose unique to us alone. We talked about that a lot. We read books, we took college courses to prepare us for marriage and family and, most important of all, we took time to pray for God's blessing. This was a very deliberate decision.

Giving life to each other is not dependent on performance. Our purpose changed; it was all about giving life, even at the expense of personal sacrifice and even when we weren't getting anything back. Our commitment to one another is not dependent on what the other person does; it is about what we promised each other on that day of ceremony. That day we promised to meet the needs of one another ahead of our own, no matter what circumstances came our way!

Covenant Is God's Secret

Covenant is God's mysterious secret to wonderful and enduring relationships. Covenant is alive and well in the heart, purposes and plans of God for this generation. For that reason, we must look at covenant through the eyes of faith and the clarifying vision of the Holy Spirit. Another reason to consider God's plan of covenant is that it brings great benefit to us and transforms our lives. In fact, the covenant life is simply the life of a true disciple of Jesus Christ.

Real, outward proof of covenant life in action is the presence of genuine truth and honesty in the relationship between a husband and a wife. If a man and woman are in covenant, then their communications with one another should demonstrate a constant level of truth and honesty no matter what circumstances they face as a married couple. The benefits of covenant include security, assurance, protection

51

and hope.

The beauty of covenant is the freedom to relinquish personal rights such as controlling your own time and money and maintaining your reputation; now you are committed to honor each other completely. That means not withholding attention, honesty or sexual intimacy from each other, making for a relationship that is secure and blessed. Even crying and using self-pity, threats, bribes and bitterness can be controlling factors that must be given up for the sake of covenant.

Covenant creates faithfulness in us individually because it births a deep desire to bring honor and joy to our covenant partner. Covenant relationships include a built-in level of personal accountability because we relate to each other with an honesty that strips away façades and falsehood. In a true covenant environment we feel free to admit our failures and recurring challenges in life because we know we won't be rejected for our honesty. Then our spouse feels free to speak the truth in love to help us overcome our failures, while walking with us through the difficulties. This is covenant living in Christ at its best.

>
>
> *The truth is, the gospel is about covenant – the good news of God's new covenant with man sealed in Christ's precious blood.*

Covenant is a God thing. The Bible clearly speaks of the blessings of walking in covenant, which include favor with God, blessed finances, security and trust, long life and health and godly character!

The truth is, the gospel is about covenant – the good news of God's new covenant with man sealed in Christ's precious blood. In fact, the Bible says:

> *For this reason Christ is the mediator of a new covenant, that those who are called may receive the promised eternal inheritance – now that he has died as a ransom to set them free from the sins committed under the first covenant.*

Hebrews 9:15, NIV

The power of God's greatest covenant with mankind is found in the death of His Son, Jesus Christ. Christ rose from the dead and now serves as the Mediator of that same covenant of grace. We must rediscover our awe and reverence for the price He paid for our freedom.

The Day We Said, "I'm Done"

The way our grandparents and great-grandparents viewed marriage has undergone erosion in succeeding generations. A seismic shift has occurred in our culture which now elevates selfishness. If most people who are getting married these days were brutally honest, their vows would probably be something like this: "I take you today to be my lawfully wedded spouse, to have and to hold until we get good and sick of each other, or until you cheat on me or fail me in some way. I love the idea of this being forever, so let's try it! Maybe we are soul mates! So as long as you're keeping me happy, I will stay with you, baby!"

Unfortunately, this kind of marriage arrangement has no guarantees or security. This is why someone invented the prenuptial agreement! Couples may say, "Until death do us part"; but really, how can they be sure?

The two of us are completely convinced that you can be sure and that there can be a guarantee. We're not talking about perfect people here; we're talking about two people who will mess up, fail, make wrong decisions and not live up to each other's expectations. But they'll always choose love, no matter what. There is a confident place of safety within marriage that can be established where the commitment is so deep that nothing will ever penetrate it. In fact, that is the true place where a relationship can thrive and spouses become best friends and best lovers.

The summer we got engaged, Bob's parents separated. No matter how old you are, the divorce of your parents stings. It was never supposed to happen. Their marriage was surviving; but who wants to live in that? Especially when your dream was to thrive and enjoy life together.

Everyone we've talked to who has traveled through the pain of divorce understands the anguish of being robbed. They think divorce is a way to get back what's theirs and get what they want.

Our message to those who are barely surviving in marriage is this: There is a third alternative. Instead of merely surviving, and instead of divorce, consider applying life-altering paradigms that reach beyond commitment and embrace covenant, the agreement that cannot be broken. Those who have chosen to do whatever it takes have discovered that the road from rock bottom can only go up. And there's resurrected life ahead! In other words, apart from covenant, we tend to focus on life today while giving no thought to how our present actions and decisions will affect the children, grandchildren and great-grandchildren of tomorrow. One of the unique qualities of biblical covenant is its ability to transfer and exponentially multiply its benefits to future generations.

What about Our Kids?

So what advice do we give our kids? How will they survive marriage in a culture where divorce is widely accepted and often expected? There's a theory that there is one special person for each of us; someone who was created especially to be our mate. According to this theory, it is our responsibility and primary prayer request for God to guide us to that one particular person. We can't leave such an important matter to chance. If we don't find Mr. or Miss "Right," we will end up marrying Mr. or Miss "Wrong" and reap a lifetime of disappointment and hardship. So, be afraid; be very afraid that you don't mess up and marry the wrong person! You must search out "the one" at all costs!

Guess what? That theory is wrong! It's as wrong as Ptolemy's ancient theory that the sun circles the earth! God has not pre-selected anyone to be your mate. There is no cosmic matchmaking chart that links Bill and Sue or Millie and Stu or anybody else. The truth is that we could have chosen any person in this world as a mate. As creatures of free will, we possess complete liberty in this area.

Does that thought rattle your paradigm? Let's look at it more closely. God is sovereign, which means He is completely self-determining. He is accountable to no one but Himself. According to His own free will God created us in His own image, making us to be like Him, and gave us dominion over the earthly realm (see Genesis 1:26-28). Because we are like God, we possess the same power of self-determination within the parameters of our earthly dominion. This is why, for example, God does not automatically or immediately intervene when we do things that are destructive to others or to our planet. He has given us dominion and we are responsible for our choices, good or bad.

As self-determining creatures we each have complete freedom to choose whomever we wish as our marriage partner; and that person possesses the same freedom. God will not choose your spouse for you. However, He will gladly and lovingly grant you wisdom, guidance and protection as you ask Him for His help. Ultimately, you cannot hold God accountable if you make a poor choice.

So how can you be sure to make a good choice? And what can you do if you have made a bad one? We want to encourage that single person who has made a list of qualifications for Mr. or Miss Right. Suppose you meet someone who scores an 8 out of 10 on your list. You immediately think, "That person can't be the one." Don't be too sure. No one is perfect. Your list should reflect your values, the things most important to you as a person. This person may not share all of them, at least not yet. But you are not the same person you were 10 years ago, either.

Having relationships is at the very center of our personhood. God made us in His image; that means we are "God-imagers." We were created to demonstrate God's image to the world around us, to reflect His nature. God is relational by nature, and we are the same way. Just as He declared that it was not good for Adam to be alone, we too find that face to face, heart to heart, person to person relationships with our own kind can end our aloneness. We need other people in order to know ourselves. We can't know ourselves in isolation. It is only as we act and interact within relationships that we come to know ourselves for who we truly are. It is when we seek to know and understand the other person that we fully discover our own identity.

A relationship is a living organism that is always changing.

First, you can never know with absolute certainty beforehand what your future will hold. Second, if you feel you made a poor choice, you have several options. You can embrace the philosophy of our divorce culture and bail out. Or you can resign yourself to your mistake by taking on a martyr mentality and trying to muddle through as best you can, snatching bits of happiness wherever you can find them. But wait; there is a third option! You can resource the benefits of being in covenant with the Lord where you embrace His grace and trust in Him to help transform your bad choice into a great marriage.

The only perfect party in a heavenly covenant is God alone. Everything and everyone else is covered by His grace. He will move heaven and earth to preserve covenant if necessary. When covenant is withheld, God will race across heaven to help because He wants to display His splendor and glory to a lost and dying world. You are His glory as you become best friends and best lovers enjoying a loving, thriving, fruitful and thoroughly satisfying marriage that will stand the test of time and weather all the storms of life.

We meet people constantly who confide in us that they have married the "wrong one." Sometimes they will say, "You don't know what it's like being married to the wrong person." Our usual response runs something like, "Yes, that may be true. Perhaps you did not choose your mate wisely. But that does not mean that he or she is not the right one for you."

How can this be? Take a moment and think about the choice you made when you married your spouse. You could have chosen any person in this world to be your mate, and you chose this person. And this person chose you. The moment you said, "I do," that person became the one for you in the eyes of God. Some entered into covenant out of pressure, or because there was a child on the way, and they think, "I should never have made this covenant." But God says that because you have entered into covenant you should respect every vow that you have made.

Covenant is why marriage is intended to be a lifelong relationship. Since God is unchanging, a covenant by its very nature is irrevocable. Unlike a contract, a covenant contains no escape clause. You may think there is no hope for your marriage, but we happen to believe there is. Why? Because we are convinced that if God can save and transform a marriage like ours, wracked by adultery and betrayal, then He can save and transform anyone's marriage, including yours. We choose to gain a new point of view. We want God's view and opinion to become our reality. This transformation does not begin with your mate changing. It begins with you. It starts with your transformed heart and new point of view.

Marriage: Contract vs. Covenant

Modern Western society views marriage more as a contract than a covenant. Unfortunately, this viewpoint has in large measure infected the church and the minds of many, many Christians. One reason for this is because there are so few examples of covenant in Western culture today. Most people, including perhaps most Christians, really have no idea of what a covenant is or how it works. Oh, we still give lip service to covenant, particularly in our wedding ceremonies; but by and large we do not understand what we are saying. Because of the pervasiveness of our secularized culture, our lips may say the word *covenant*, but our minds are thinking, *contract*.

A covenant, as we have already mentioned, is irrevocable. It testifies to a permanent relationship. A contract is different. Contracts generally are issued for specific, clearly defined purposes under tightly specified conditions and for a limited but precisely spelled-out time frame. A contract can be amended, modified, expanded, reduced or even cancelled as the need arises. Once the terms of the contract are met, the contract dissolves.

Is it any wonder, then, that our culture of divorce thrives as it does? If we view marriage as nothing more than a contract, then if things do not go as we expected we can simply cancel the contract, go on our merry way and somewhere down the line strike up a new contract with somebody else. More and more people in our society are simply abandoning the contract altogether, choosing to participate in an easily dissolved relationship that dispenses with the inconvenience of a formal, legalized agreement.

Covenant, on the other hand, has a refreshing, reassuring permanence about it. God has made a covenant with us that He will never leave us or forsake us (Hebrews 13:5). He has promised always to love us, accept us and forgive us. Not only does He make this solemn oath to us, but it is actually impossible for God to break His covenant. To do so would mean to break faithfulness, and God is always faithful. The faithfulness of God and the unbreakable nature of His covenant bring us great comfort, security, peace and amazing freedom. God's unconditional love for us will never change. This makes Him completely approachable and fully reliable. What could be more beautiful than that?

It is this same covenant that is symbolically shadowed through our ceremony of holy matrimony. That is why marriage is supposed to be a lifelong commitment; it reflects the permanence of God's covenant with man. When we pledge our wedding vows, we promise to be there for each other through the good, the bad and the ugly. We promise to continue loving each other through sickness and through hard times as well as in good times. Then we seal the promise with the words, "until death us do part."

So what happens when one of those within the covenant breaks the vow? We have seen this firsthand. This is exactly what happened when I, Audrey, committed adultery after seventeen years of marriage. In my vows I had promised to keep myself and give myself to Bob alone. Yet I directly violated our covenant and robbed Bob of what was rightfully his.

In cases like this, even most Christians provide a way out for the offended spouse; here we can see the influence of secular society on

Christian thinking. The argument goes like this: "Hey, she cheated on you; the Bible itself says that you are now free to go. Divorce is okay in the case of adultery. Let her walk. Better yet, walk away yourself and let her deal with the travesty!"

We are both so thankful that we received true biblical counsel! When the pastor counseling Bob gave direction, he asked Bob a direct question: "When we sin against God, does He break covenant with us?" The obvious answer is, "Never!" This pastor and counselor then challenged Bob to be a covenant keeper. Keeping covenant is so different from keeping a contract. A contract says, "I'll keep my end of the deal as long as you keep yours." The moment one or the other of the holders of the contract messes up in any way, the contract is null and void. Cancelled. Dissolved. And thus we have "no fault" divorce.

A covenant keeper, however, says, "I will keep my part of the covenant regardless of whether or not you keep yours." This is why God never gives up on trying to redeem even the most seemingly difficult, painful and hopeless of situations. He is a covenant-keeping God and will never abandon His children. His children may abandon Him, but God always remains faithful.

Wherever you are right now in your marital struggles, no matter how dark and grim everything seems, you can turn it around if you gain a new point of view! God wants you to be completely fulfilled and fully satisfied with your spouse and with your marriage. Submit yourself humbly to Him, let Him transform your heart and watch your relationship revive. You don't have to give up on your dreams. You don't have to settle for less than the best. You can go all the way to "more than enough"!

***

10 Out of 10: Bob's Turn

I'll always remember a drive through the country just a few short weeks after Audrey told me that she had committed adultery. I was with a highly respected pastor and friend, and confided in him about our situation. Audrey was pregnant and we now had many difficult decisions to make. My friend proceeded to tell me that his wife had had an emotional, although not sexual, affair and that he had to come to grips with the fact that they would never have a perfect marriage. They would survive; but he was resigned to settle for a marriage that was, at best, an 8 out of 10.

I gripped the steering wheel tightly as everything inside of me screamed, "No! This can't be! If God is real, and if He loves me, and if He's everything He's told me He is, then I want it all! I don't want to just survive in this marriage; I want to thrive! I want a 10 out of 10!"

Faith rose up in the midst of impossible circumstances. At that time Audrey and I were not doing well at all. We were desperate and scared. But we knew we needed God, and He is the God of covenant who honors covenant. He is the God of "more than enough."

This idea will challenge many to the very core of their beliefs, because it is a new point of view! You would not believe all the phone calls I received at the very beginning from other pastors and national leaders who told me that because of Audrey's act of adultery I had every right to leave. Some of you may not understand or agree with everything we say here regarding covenant; but putting aside your personal point of view and just speaking relationally, I want what's best for my present circumstances: for my wife, for my children and for future generations. Because of that, I want to learn God's ways. In learning God's ways I experienced His unconditional love.

Audrey and I have had the tremendous opportunity in recent years of ministering with Craig and Jan Hill of Family Foundations in conducting international covenant marriage retreats. In this circle, many have thanked me for being a "covenant keeper." In the beginning I wasn't familiar with the term, and I wasn't even passionate about covenant the way I am now. I knew I was doing what was best. However, it wasn't because I knew the depths of covenant, but was based more upon a relational decision of walking with the Lord and understanding His heart for our family and His ultimate desire for our very best. I was a broken individual wanting to understand and know God's ways.

Many of you may be at the very beginning of a journey to reestablish covenant in your own heart, in your home and in your marriage. As a result of embracing truth in this area, you will better understand the covenant that God has made with you. This will give you a new point of view of His ever-pursuing love.

***

Covenant Covers Future Generations: Audrey

Everyone wants a sense of family, of belonging. Either we're going to attach ourselves to groups and clubs with people of like mind searching for that lost sense of belonging, or we'll listen to the lies of worthlessness and retreat to a place of isolation and alienation. Young people want to show and demonstrate their loyalty to one another. They're after an outward expression of covenant, hungry for covenantal security and bonding.

Speaking of children and the future, the rewards of covenant keeping extend from generation to generation. Had Bob chosen not to preserve our marriage, our children could easily have been wounded for life by my act of adultery. Because of our ordeal they might have embraced a bitterness and cynicism that could have negatively impacted their own marriages and all of their other relationships. Instead, the Lord showed Bob a way to protect the children and preserve their sense of security.

When Bob told our children about the adultery and the resulting pregnancy, he covered me. I mean, he literally placed a blanket over me as he told them how I had sinned. In the same breath he promised them that we would stay together through this, and that our family was not breaking up. Even as they first heard the bad news, our children also heard the strength and peace of covenant in Bob's words. He told them that he was doing exactly what our Father in heaven does whenever we mess up. He covers us. He doesn't shame or expose us. Instead,

He holds us close and heals us with His unconditional love and whispers words of comfort. *"I will never leave you or forsake you."*

Participating in covenant invites the holy presence of Almighty God to bless and preserve an entire family for generations to come. Today our children are not fearful of marriage. Rather than carrying a lot of baggage of bitterness, they anticipate wonderful abundant lives of more than enough. That is the beauty, the miracle, of covenant. Covenant is God's idea for human relationships. And there has never been a better one!

Irreconcilable Differences

We live today in a pervasive culture of divorce. For decades the phrase "irreconcilable differences" has been a popular route to divorce for married couples who have given up the fight. Sometimes it is simply another way of saying, "Nothing bad has happened; we just don't love each other anymore, and we definitely don't want to live together any longer. We're too different. We're better apart than together."

In many cases "irreconcilable differences" is a divorcing couple's way of saying that they are not up to the challenge of working through their conflicts and pressing through to genuine reconciliation. Pride may prevent them from acknowledging their mistakes. The memory of betrayal or of harsh and hateful words may sting too much. Anger over shattered trust or unfulfilled expectations may have nurtured a root of bitterness that has poisoned the relationship. The stress of repeated conflict may have sapped their energy, enthusiasm and confidence, wearying them to the point of giving up.

If the ship of your relationship has collided with the rocks of conflict and is foundering in the breakers, ready to go under, you have to face some tough questions: Can this relationship be saved? Do I want to save it? Am I willing to do whatever it takes, no matter how hard or painful, to draw back from the brink, rebuild the relationship and rekindle the passion? Am I prepared to go the distance, to press through for full healing and reconciliation?

No one can answer these questions but you. If you and your mate are going through stormy waters right now you may wonder if your relationship can survive, or if it's even worth fighting for. Take it from us: It is! Our marriage survived adultery and an unexpected pregnancy. Today we are happier and our marriage is stronger and deeper and richer than it has ever been. No matter the condition of your relationship, there is hope if you will reach out and take hold of it. Don't throw away your marriage – instead of fighting against each other, begin fighting for each other.

> *No matter the condition of your relationship, there is hope if you will reach out and take hold of it.*

Nevertheless, what you do is up to you. To reconcile or not to reconcile; the choice is yours. And therein lays the key. Reconciliation won't happen by accident. You must deliberately choose to reconcile. The road to reconciliation begins with a revelation or, as we've been saying, a new point of view.

Called to Reconcile

Reconciliation with God has a deeper dimension than simply being made right personally with Him. God's invitation for us to be reconciled with Him carries with it a call to join with Him in the work of reconciling others in the same way. Let's examine a portion of Scripture from Second Corinthians that directly relates to this concept of reconciliation:

> *All this newness of life is from God, who brought us back to himself through what Christ did.* **And God has given us the task of reconciling people to him.** *For God was in Christ, reconciling the world to himself, no longer counting people's sins against them.* **This is the wonderful message he has given us to tell others.**
>
> Second Corinthians 5:18-19, emphasis added

Now that we are reconciled to God in Christ, God has assigned to us the task, or ministry, of reconciling others to Him. This is both a wonderful privilege and an awesome responsibility. Essentially, this means sharing with others what Christ has done for us and helping them to understand that He can do the same for them.

In Christ, then, we are reconcilers by nature and by calling. Consider the implications. This means that not only are we to seek to reconcile other people with God, but we also have the responsibility to seek reconciliation in every area and relationship of our lives! In other words, pursuing reconciliation in our marriage or with our children or in any other relationship is just as much a fulfillment of this Scripture as is sharing the message of Christ with someone. Whenever we do the work of reconciliation, at any level, we do the work of Christ because He is the great Reconciler. Reconciliation brings peace. Jesus said, *"God blesses those who work for peace, for they will be called the children of God"* (Matthew 5:9).

A Bit of Heaven on Earth

If you're afraid that your marriage is too far gone to be saved, or that there is too much hurt, too much betrayal or too many angry words to go back, consider this: Jesus the great Reconciler wants to see your marriage reconciled even more than you do. When people are in covenant, it is common for them to say, "Look, I will not betray you." Why do they say this? It is because covenant is intricately intertwined with trust, faithfulness and integrity. One of the root promises behind every covenant is in these words. "I will never betray you." Biblical covenant deals with your past, present and future. That is because God Himself accepts the past, believes in the present and hopes for the future.

Keeping covenant with your spouse is a way to participate in heavenly living. It does not matter what has happened between the two of you or what may be going on right now. Please believe us when we tell you that your decision to keep covenant with your spouse will bring a deep and genuine sense of peace and satisfaction to your heart even in the midst of disappointment, turmoil and conflict. How do we know? Partly by personal experience; partly because covenant keeping means being faithful, and faithfulness is a quality of a satisfied heart.

So if you long for a satisfied heart, learn to cherish the one you have – cherish your spouse as he or she is right now, not as you hope he or she will be someday. And stop dreaming that someone better might come along. There is no one better, no one more right for you than the person you are married to now. Because of covenant, that person who shares your bed and your life is the right one for you. So take heed of the counsel from Proverbs that says: "Let your wife [or husband] be a fountain of blessing for you. Rejoice in the wife [or husband] of your youth" (see Proverbs 5:18).

Your spouse is a gift from God in your life. He may not have made the choice for you, but once you chose and entered into covenant He endorsed your choice. And now He desires to anoint your marriage with His grace and bless you through your spouse and your spouse through you. Treat your spouse like a gift and that is what he or she will become to you. Of course your spouse is not perfect, but then neither are you. None of us is. But your spouse is perfect for you.

There is no one in this world anointed to love me the way Bob is. The moment we made covenant together and pledged, "until death do us part," heaven took notice and stamped "It's done!" next to our names in God's covenant record book. Ever since then, if I ever feel that I am not loved, I am just focusing on the wrong thing!

We remember sitting in a booth at a restaurant years ago with another couple. Unable to have children of their own, this other couple asked us for advice about adoption. "Should we make the effort to start a family?" they asked. "How do the two of you feel about being parents?" What a question! The joys and rewards of having children far outweigh the cost! Our answer was, "Parents who view their kids as a problem usually have problem kids. The more you view your kids as a blessing, the more they become a blessing!" Of course, that is a broad and generalized statement, but we need to think about the joys and privileges of being family, spouses and children together.

When a woman sees someone else's husband who appears to be amazing in a certain area, she must remember quickly that her own husband is the perfect person to care for her, protect her and provide for her. A woman whose husband doesn't make a lot of money may see another man as a much better provider. What she doesn't see, however, is that the "better provider" may be a workaholic who is seldom around to give quality time to his family. Another woman sees a man who is charming and funny and entertaining, and begins comparing him to her humorless, lackluster husband. Yet she fails to see the control issues and other characteristics that make this charmer impossible to live with. There is no such thing as a perfect spouse; only a spouse who is perfect for you. And that's the one you're with, even if it looks like a long shot!

A Well-Tended Garden: Audrey

It was a beautiful spring day in Canada. The snow had melted and the aroma of growth and life was in the air! I couldn't wait to get started on my garden. All my kids were quite small at the time, and one of them had managed to bring a cardboard box outside that was full of shipping chips – those little white Styrofoam chips that weigh absolutely nothing.

They must have wanted to play in the "snow," because those chips ended up all over the backyard! I wasn't sure how to deal with them. They were too light to rake; if I hauled out the shop vac, I'd pick up a lot more than the chips.

While I pondered what to do, the doorbell rang. A friend of mine, with her kids in tow, arrived for a quick cup of coffee. As I watched her kids and mine together (at least five of them) I got a grand idea. Handing each child a brown paper lunch bag, I told them that I would give each of them a quarter for every bag they filled up with those little white chips. They were absolutely thrilled! My impossible clean-up challenge suddenly became an adventure as each child raced the others into the backyard.

My friend and I were still enjoying our coffee when the first child arrived with a knock at the back door. She was about two years old and wasn't just a girl—she was a princess! She always wore dresses and fluffy white socks with glossy dress shoes. With a huge smile on her face, she proudly handed us her brown paper bag full of—doggy doo-doo!

The little princess was too excited about her "bag" to worry about her dirty hands, shoes and socks. And we were laughing too hard to be upset about anything. Forget the twenty-five cents; she got a dollar for that clean-up job!

Getting rid of that doggy-mess was the next thing I would have to contend with, but like anyone who gardens I knew there will be weeds, thorns, thistles and stormy weather. But it's all worth it for the reward of that beautiful aroma, the gorgeous array of colors and textures and the excitement of watching the growth take place day by day.

In the Book of Ezekiel, God speaks of giving us a new heart with new desires and promises to put a new spirit in us (Ezekiel 36:25-27). He says, *"And when I bring you back, people will say, 'This godforsaken land is now like Eden's garden! The ruined cities now have strong walls, and they are filled with people!' "* (Ezekiel 36:35)

I love walls. Within walls there is safety, protection and, best of all, freedom. Strong walls mean concrete boundaries where there is no guessing, but much peace. When I think of a marriage that is strong, I think of one with strong walls; walls of protection and security. And that is the role of covenant.

Just as walls surround and secure a garden, so covenant surrounds and secures a marriage. Covenant creates the perfect environment for relationship to flourish and thrive. Without covenant, one bad storm might be all it would take to destroy all the beautiful growth and tear everything down to its roots. Without the protective walls of covenant, the enemy could come in little by little and devour the growth until it became impossible to regain strength.

Jesus is the master Gardener, and ultimately He wants your marriage to be like a well-watered garden. He wants to restore your relationship to its original intent. Begin dreaming of what this marriage could look like. Imagine the garden of Eden and the paradise that was created for man's enjoyment.

In your future lies the potential for a marriage just like this:

Replenishing...restored

Beautiful...satisfying

Solitude....fulfillment

Rest...safety

Fruitfulness...lushness

Life...enjoyment

Nakedness...no shame

Only people who walk in covenant with God can fulfill this divine mystery. The modern church has difficulty in making sense of the manifold wisdom of God when it doesn't understand covenant. It is more likely to fall back on its comfortable traditions rather than teach submission to one another, unity and covenant living. God is out to change things in the church. Divine covenant has a way of saying, "I'm going to give you far more than you will ever be able to give back to Me."

The Lord is ready to hear your prayers for blessing and ready to grant your request. Choose to stay in your covenant relationship and trust God with your spouse. Your prayers for a marriage that is like the garden of Eden will bear fruit in time. It all begins with the walls of covenant. Established. Strong. Thick. Deep. Deliberate. Never moving.

As you are joined in covenant, you are much better together than apart. When fighting the enemy, if one person can put a thousand to flight, then two can send entire legions fleeing. As for Bob and me, we have covenanted that we will not fight against each other, but fight for each other. What God has joined together, no man will put asunder. We are together forever and will not participate with the spirit of divorce by ever bringing that word into our home, whether through threats, jokes or temptation. We are together until death parts us. That is not imprisonment; it is freedom! We know that we will be loved for life, and loved to life.

Heart Revelation: The Tough Questions

Have you committed in your heart never to mention divorce as an option?

Have you been fighting against each other, instead of fighting for each other?

When you got married, did you understand that the covenant you were making was for life? Can you grasp that reality now?

Have you experienced the sting of divorce? Are you willing to ask God's forgiveness for breaking covenant in order to embrace the relationship you are presently in?

Have you questioned your choice of marriage partner, wondering if you married the wrong person? Are you willing to embrace the covenant that you made, understanding and affirming that the one you are with is indeed the anointed person from God to be with you for life?

With an attitude of contract rather than covenant, have you let your spouse know that he or she has not held up his or her end of the deal?

Have you used self-pity, threats, bribes or punishment to control your spouse? Are you willing to lay those down?

Have you withheld attention and honesty from your spouse in order to get your own way?

Will you commit to whatever it takes to have a 10/10 marriage?

When are the times you haven't covered your spouse, but rather exposed, judged or ridiculed him or her?

Are you secure in your relationship with God? Have you been reconciled to God through Jesus Christ?

Heart Transformation: The Truth Established

We are married for life. There is no need to mention divorce, for God has given us His grace, which is sufficient for whatever we're facing. (See Ephesians 2:6-10.)

God is One who fights for us, but calls us to love one another as our highest calling. (See First John 4:7-8.)

As I stay in covenant with my spouse, I am inviting blessings for my family for generations to come. (See Psalm 100:5.)

I am married to the one who is most anointed in God's sight to fulfill my needs, as I fulfill his or her needs. (See Philippians 2:1-5.)

With God's help, we can enjoy a satisfied married life as He intended it to be. He supplies our needs in every way! (See Philippians 4:19.)

God's protection, favor, life and blessings surround our marriage and we are protected, knowing that we will be together forever (See Psalm 5:11-12.)

If I am already in a second marriage (or later), I am free to receive God's grace and forgiveness for breaking covenant. Because of His life, I can receive His blessing for the marriage I am in right now. (See Psalm 103:10-12.)

There's no fear or judgment in God, but grace, mercy and unconditional love. (See Second Timothy 1:7.)

Prayer

Father in heaven, I invite Your presence into our marriage. There are things I've said and done that don't reflect Your covenant; please forgive me. Forgive me for when I've used manipulation and control in my marriage. Lord, I'm thankful that You are a covenantal God and that You never leave us. Thank You for my spouse. Thank You that he or she is the most anointed to love me!

[And for those who are in difficult circumstances...]

Lord, I'm so worried about my life. Things are not going as I'd planned at all. This was not in the deal when I got married. I don't feel loved or cherished. I don't feel honored or appreciated. And I can't do anything to fix anyone around me. It's so frustrating! I know that the only chance I have of being saved from all of this is to let You catch me when I fall and carry me. I know You didn't ask me to do this alone, and You never asked me to fix anyone. Help me take my refuge in You. Help me to let go and really trust You.

Thank You, God, for never holding anything back from me. I know you're not punishing me. I know that no good thing will You withhold from those who walk uprightly. The power of sin is broken over my life, and nothing, absolutely nothing can separate me from Your love.

Secure Commitment: Even after it was lost...

After an intense session during a marriage conference, we sat down for lunch with several other couples. We had never met them, but were happy to get to know some new friends. At the end of the mealtime there was only one couple left sitting with us, and we will never forget their story.

As we began to ask questions, we found out that they had been separated for five years. They were sitting together at lunch – that alone was a miracle! They had been living a few miles from each other. He had a mistress, and they continued to run their family business together. Their relationship had become strictly business; there was barely even a hope that they would one day join hearts again.

It was during this weekend that they heard about hope and began to take hold of it. Their faith was strengthened as they learned about the power of covenant. By the end of the weekend they had renewed their vows in the presence of their grown children, who had been praying diligently for their parents to get back together. What a life-changing, life-affirming blessing it is to walk in covenant with God and with one another!

3

SWEET CONVERSATION

You can't do things differently until you see things differently. So, as we begin, remind yourself that you may very well need a new point of view when it comes to communication. If from where you stand things just are not working all that well, try moving to higher ground to gain a new perspective.

Ultimately, learning the language of love is all about the journey to intimacy. Good communication is especially critical here. As soon as we say the word "intimacy," the breakdown in understanding begins. Because men and women are created differently, they think differently. A husband and wife may both speak of intimacy, yet be worlds apart in both understanding and expectations.

If we struggle to communicate, we need to see the process differently. We need a new point of view that will help us solve the daily communication problems we face. And God is ready and willing to give us that new perspective. He wants to give us a much greater understanding. He wants to give us confidence that we can reach the one who is closest to us, as well as those around us. (See Mark 16:15.)

What marriage book would be complete without a chapter on communication? This is a great challenge for us; we don't wish merely to transfer information, but rather for you to capture the meaning of what is being written, resulting in true communication.

The body of Christ has been charged with the responsibility of reaching the whole world with His good news. What a huge goal! More personally, each one of us wants to see Christ lived out in each of our relationships. We can find this challenge exhilarating; but when it comes to those closest to us, we sometimes think we could get a better response by talking to a brick wall!

You have probably heard that only 15% of human communication occurs through the words we speak. The other 85% occurs through body language, tone of voice and facial expressions. All of us have experienced discerning someone's mood simply by that person's presence. Without a word being spoken, that person's overall demeanor communicates volumes. Every couple has their own language. We call it "heart talk." We have sounds, whistles and words that are personal just for us. Good communication is a skill that every married couple must develop constantly and pursue deliberately. Statistically speaking, the breakdown of communication is the most often cited reason associated with divorce. And so much of it happens by accident! Our own baggage of insecurities causes us to "hear" something completely differently than what was intended.

So let's learn to communicate God's way. He is truly the master Communicator and His methods work. We don't have to take our cue from the world and mask over it with a thin Christian veneer. Let's put away our romance novels and turn off the television. Let's discover God's Word and be taught in His ways!

God instituted covenant as a way to put heavenly stability to earthly instability. Covenant is a principle, a heavenly stronghold that can only be entered through the door of truth. Most couples seem to build their relationships on likeness or shared ideas of what they want in life. Covenant requires us to be involved in the lives of our loved ones. God's Word, our supreme guide to covenant living, puts it this way:

Instead, speaking the truth in love, we will in all things grow up into Him who is the Head, that is, Christ. From him the whole body,

joined and held together by every supporting ligament, grows and builds itself up in love, as each part does its work.
Ephesians 4:15-16, NIV

The Bible says that when we discover and know Him who is truth, the truth will set us free. The truth may hurt, but those in covenant must prefer the painful truth to the comfortable lie. Covenant is perceived, received and lived from the heart, not the head.

The Gospel of John begins: *"In the beginning was the Word…and the Word was God"* (John 1:1). God is so synonymous with communication that Scripture refers to Him as the Word, the *Logos* of life. As impossible as it is to separate the God of the Bible from love, for God is love, it is equally impossible to separate God from communication, for God is communication.

When God created human beings, male and female, He walked and talked with them in the garden of Eden on a daily basis. God took the rib out of Adam and formed Eve into a beautiful, precious person. She was to be Adam's encouragement and helpmeet so that they would fulfill their destiny together. A man should leave his mother and father and become one flesh with his wife. Adam and Eve were both naked and not ashamed. There's a premise for some sweet conversation! When mankind participated with sin, sin brought separation and broken communication. But God committed Himself even to the death of His Son to ensure that relationship and communication might be restored.

God sent His prophets with His Word. He inspired the writing of His Word. He even supernaturally wrote His Word on stone and gave it to Moses. He sent His own Son Jesus, the living Word, to personally embody and bear His message. Why would God go through all this trouble and so much more just to communicate with a rebellious people like us? Why all the commitment? The answer is very clear: because He loves us. God is love, and love has to communicate.

The Bible shows us a picture of God's heart in communication.

Throughout the Book of Hosea the Lord says: "I tried this and you wouldn't listen to Me. I tried that and still you refused to listen. I wept over you and agonized, and you continued to ignore me" (authors' paraphrase).

God invested in man tremendous power over his own destiny. And while there is no barrier so great that it prevents God from communicating with His creation, once He has communicated, the decision of whether to heed the word still lies in the domain of each individual. The greatest and most terrifying attribute of the human race is our personal will. What an awesome responsibility and, for many, a fearful burden, we carry with our own personal choice.

The Mark of a Friend Is Open Communication

I no longer call you servants, because a master doesn't confide in his servants. Now you are my friends, since I have told you everything the Father told me.
John 15:15

Here Jesus indicates that one of the marks of friendship is communication. In the Father's house we are sons and daughters. However, we often prefer to be known as God's servants. Why? Because servanthood requires a much lower level of commitment and intimacy. We can distance ourselves emotionally if we view ourselves as servants.

This is similar to the attitude of the children of Israel, who insisted that Moses speak with God rather than God speaking directly to them. The end result was that Moses came to know the ways of God while the people saw only His miracles. As great as God's miracles are, our desire should be to know His heart. That will require us to get close – really close – and intimate. Intimacy is intimidating by its very nature. If you have never been intimidated by God, then you probably haven't been very close to Him. At times it will even feel a little too close for comfort; but that's when you know you are communicating at the level He desires.

Jesus offers us open, unguarded communication as His standard of friendship. Becoming best friends and best lovers transpires into deep intimacy. This takes place through transparency. Our intimacy with one another is largely determined by our intimacy with God. The beauty, honor and respect with which we walk individually with God determines the unity, harmony and beauty we will have with each other. Transparency with God, or with our spouse, will provide God access into our garden, where He will walk and talk with us face to face and where we will be in His powerful and beautiful presence.

There is purity, beauty and holiness in this relationship. Nothing is hidden. Everything is completely open, flowing with each other's desires, each other's purpose, each other's vision and each other's direction. That level of transparency, respect and honor draws God's presence into its midst! We can live in that kind of beauty, that tangible presence of God, as we work on getting transparency flowing in our relationship.

The Battle to Communicate

For we are not fighting against people made of flesh and blood, but against the evil rulers and authorities of the unseen world, against those mighty powers of darkness who rule this world, and against wicked spirits in the heavenly realms.
Ephesians 6:12

We use God's mighty weapons, not mere worldly weapons, to knock down the Devil's strongholds. With these weapons we break down every proud argument that keeps people from knowing God. With these weapons we conquer their rebellious ideas, and we teach them to obey Christ.
Second Corinthians 10:4-5

The greatest gift we can give God is to believe Him. Our greatest temptation, even as believers, is to not believe God. The enemy's strategy is to destroy the image and character of God in mankind and return him to a place of loneliness. Satan wants to destroy all of our relationships by cutting the lines of communication. The greatest challenge you will ever face in your marriage is being willing to deepen your level of communication. The day you decide to stop working at communicating is the day you begin to walk away from your marriage.

>
> *The greatest gift we can give God is to believe Him. Our greatest temptation, even as believers, is to not believe God.*

Understand this: Satan doesn't necessarily hate you or your marriage. He hates God and he hates our capacity to manifest God's image. There is a hurting world out there, desperate for us to communicate to them the light, life and love of God that we so freely talk about. It reminds us of the saying, "I can't hear what you are saying; your actions are too loud." We cannot display God to those around us if we cannot communicate.

It's time to pray. This is not a last-ditch effort; prayer is the most we can do. The place of prayer is where we not only let our requests be known, but also where we find God's peace (Philippians 4:6-7). Let's put our minds in Christ before we put our mouths in motion (First Corinthians 2:16). We must take our authority in Jesus, and in the place of prayer defuse the enemy's schemes to disrupt our communication efforts. Whenever you enter the place of prayer, remind yourself that God has an opinion. You can always overcome Adam and Eve's mistake of doubt: "Did God really say...?" Just ask Him!

Sending Meaningful Conversation

> *The seed that fell on the hard path represents those who hear the Good News about the Kingdom and don't understand it. Then the evil one comes and snatches the seed away from their hearts.*
> Matthew 13:19

"Wait! That's not what I said!" How many times have we spoken these words while quickly trying to say the same thing in another way? The only thing we accomplish is to dig a deeper hole for ourselves that lays us bare.

The goal of communication is to convey meaningful content from one person to another. Sending the message is only half the battle. The message must be received and understood. Much of our communication is miscommunication. It is all too easy to be thinking and planning internally and be so thorough with our plans that we fail to communicate properly with those who are there to help us. This results in the common complaint, "We need better communication!"

Communication is not merely hearing and repeating words. Communication is meaning. It is not so much the words we use, but the understanding our listeners receive. Unless we successfully convey our meaning, we have failed to communicate. Hearing words is not communication. Successful communication occurs when mutual understanding is exchanged.

We have all experienced those moments while reading our Bibles when the words seemed to jump off the page with a meaning much deeper than what we had seen before. It is in those moments that we really receive the Word of the Lord. We can read His Word, but it is the Holy Spirit who makes it come alive and conveys to us His meaning and understanding. When the meanings of Christ's words and actions are alive to us, then we can give that understanding away.

God chose to communicate from a ground level. Jesus came alongside us and identified with our weakness. "I understand your temptations; I'm not ashamed of your weaknesses. I don't condemn you. I will help you." Intolerance is a by-product of our denial of our own weakness. Too quickly we judge others by their appearance or actions. So easily we play the part of the accuser and leave those who need to be loved and restored on the outside looking in.

One of the greatest mistakes we make in communication is focusing on how different we are, creating a great canyon between ourselves and those we wish to reach. This is not a godly style of communication. No matter how wide the gap between you and the other person, there is always a place where you can communicate with your spouse; a point of contact to achieve a union of your hearts. Find those similarities – the things you share, the passions you have in common – and the communication will begin!

> *All praise to the God and Father of our Lord Jesus Christ. He is the source of every mercy and the God who comforts us. He comforts us in all our troubles so that we can comfort others. When others are troubled, we will be able to give them the same comfort God has given us*
> Second Corinthians 1:3-4

If we accept the daily suffering of overcoming temptations as Jesus did, then the most important key to effective communication will be ours. We can comfort others with the comfort Jesus has given us.

The cost of Jesus-style communication is personal humility and a willingness to lay down our lives. You can't reach anyone you don't love, and you can't love those you don't identify with.

***

Heart talk is part of the language of love. And the heart of heart talk is truth. In the Meisner marriage today there are no secrets between us. That is one of our safeguards. After I, Audrey, confessed my adultery, Bob began interrogating me relentlessly for all the details. Thoroughly shamed, I told him everything. It was horrible and degrading. Part of our reconciliation is that we both have learned to desire truth on a daily basis! With truth prevailing, we leave little room for the enemy to deceive us. The upside to this is that we have found out many fun things about each other along the way. It's like that well known definition of a friend: someone who knows absolutely everything about you and still loves you.

***

Getting to that place of total truth and vulnerability in a relationship can be a tricky thing. That is why many couples never get there. We all have secrets that no one else knows about: our private thoughts, imaginations and fantasies. And there are some things that should stay private. Truth telling is important, but should always be done carefully with discernment and discretion. Deciding what is important to tell, as well as the right time to tell, is absolutely critical. No matter how noble your motive, careless truth telling can become a weapon of the enemy to inflict unnecessary hurt and pain.

Your motive for speaking the truth and pursuing honesty and transparency is critical for success, for a wrong motive will usually backfire. Why do you want to bare your heart to your spouse? If you are seeking a deeper relationship, that is a good thing. On the other hand, if you are motivated by a desire to clear your conscience or a desire for revenge that will hurt your spouse, you will do more harm than good. These reveal a selfish motive, and selfishness has no part in the language of love.

Before approaching your spouse with the secrets of your heart, pray about it. Confide in the Lord your desire for total transparency with your spouse. Ask Him to purify your heart, confessing sin and seeking forgiveness if necessary. Ask that He might give you the right words to say and to reveal to you the proper timing. Depending on the magnitude of your offense (adultery, pornography addiction, gambling addiction, and so on) and the level of estrangement that currently exists between the two of you, don't expect an instant forgiveness. All of this may be news to your spouse, who will need time to process it. The journey to wholeness and healing is often a long road. It was for us.

But the goal – a relationship characterized by open, honest, heart to heart communication – is worth every ounce of effort expended to achieve it. Heart to heart communication occurs when there are no obstacles between you either in your words or your actions. You connect at a deep level and your words carry truth, feeling and reality. Sometimes a marriage falters because of years of accumulated obstacles over unresolved issues: irritation, frustration, disgust, lack of respect, jealousy, grievances, abuse, infidelity, dishonesty, selfishness. All of these will cause you to close your hearts to each other and, while you may continue to live in the same house together, in reality the two of you are worlds apart. Heart talk will bring you back together.

***

During the deep dark times of our restoration process I, Bob, would express my feelings, thoughts and fears. This was important for me, not because I thought Audrey would have answers for me, but so that she might gain some understanding of what I was going through and that I might receive some comfort. As time went on, I began to preface our times of talking by saying, "What I have to say may hurt, but that is not my intention at all."

It's absolutely necessary that we develop a healthy way of expressing our thoughts and emotions to each other. I can't state it often enough: If you don't have a healthy way of expressing your thoughts and emotions to each other, of speaking and being heard, then everything else will ultimately crumble.

***

Talk to Me Straight

In order to have a successful marriage you have to make yourself an expert in communication. You have to try to understand what your partner is saying on a simple level as well as trying to analyze the underlying message or desire. You must understand that the two of you are creating your own language of love.

Men, what do you say as she's spinning in the mirror, pressing her tummy and looking at her backside and then pops the question, "Does my butt look big?" If you don't already know the answer, it's "No!" The last thing a woman wants to hear when she complains about her weight is a suggestion for a new diet plan. Actually, the last thing she probably wants to hear is, "Yes dear, you do need to slim down a little!" Neither does she want just sympathetic ear (just when a man thinks he's mastered the art of good listening). What she really wants is for her husband to say, "You look hot!" "You look thin!" "You look so young!"

Ladies, don't expect your man to operate at a continual level of divine inspiration. If there's a special gift you want for your birthday, point it out and say, "I would really like that for my birthday." Men, please take mental note and, if need be, write it down. You may respond, "But what about the surprise when she opens it?" Don't worry; she'll be impressed that you listened and cared enough to get her what she really wanted. As trivial as this all may seem, it will save the agony of the man having to choose a gift and spare you both needless pain. It works both ways: Maybe he doesn't want a butter dish this year. (It's true, I bought Bob a butter dish for his birthday last year. ... Hey, he didn't like the little salad plate I was using!)

Developing Transparency

Many people are afraid to be transparent. They fear that if their true self is known, people won't like them and will reject them. The same is true with vulnerability. Once you make yourself vulnerable you open yourself up to be wounded, and who wants that? Being wounded once can make you gun-shy about opening up again. Nevertheless, we have to address these issues because transparency and vulnerability are essential characteristics of a happy, thriving and fruitful marriage. They lie at the very core of becoming best friends and best lovers.

Part of learning the language of love is learning how to be transparent and vulnerable without fear. Let's face it: if you are having marital problems – if there is anger, hostility, bitterness or mistrust between the two of you – the last thing that you probably feel like doing is being transparent or vulnerable with each other. Learning the language of love is a journey toward intimacy, and true intimacy always involves complete transparency, willing vulnerability and total honesty. That's a mighty tall order for any married couple, troubled or not!

So how do you get there? How do you move from estrangement to intimacy? From superficial conversation to open, soul-connecting dialogue? From fear and mistrust to confident, open honesty? How do you restore love that seems to have been lost somewhere? One way to begin is by realizing that, as the principle of this chapter indicates, *love is a language*. And language involves communication.

Sometimes we're confronted by the fact that there are things in our hearts that are hidden. If we have those things, we're going to walk in tricky deception. Once we've told one lie, we have to tell another in order to get out of the first one. We don't want to tell the whole truth. This easily becomes a lifestyle. That cycle won't be broken without a radical pursuit of transparency.

***

The road to adultery that I walked was preceded by months of hiding my thoughts and feelings. If I had been honest and transparent with Bob from the beginning, I would have been protected from following through with what was in my heart. Why didn't I tell him earlier? At first, it was because I didn't think it was a big deal. It was just little things, like enjoying another person's compliments, and looking forward to seeing him. Secondly, it was because I enjoyed the attention and my selfish nature wanted it to continue. I'm saddened that I let selfishness rule my heart to the point that I participated with sexual infidelity and the betrayal of Bob. Being transparent could have saved years of painful recovery.

Bob did not discover the affair; I told him about it. I was absolutely, positively convinced that the secret would drive a wedge between us. I knew enough about transparency to realize that every day there would be opportunities for Bob to discover that hidden secret inside me. I would have to be deceptive and tricky on a daily basis, even after the affair ended. Some people go about for years after adultery trying to keep the secret covered up. Whenever there are secrets between you, the first casualty is intimacy.

***

This is why most couples have a side by side relationship. They walk parallel lives so that any secrets between them can remain hidden. The words they communicate to each other may be correct, but what is flowing out of their spirits is confusion. An impure or divided heart eventually produces confused and conflicted communication. Pure hearts that carry no hidden things will no longer communicate confusion, but harmony.

God will always bless your efforts at transparency, whatever the cost. Pledge yourself to do whatever needs to be done to bring a greater level of God's presence into your lives and into your home.

Timing is extremely important when it comes to confessing the truth that is in your heart. There are no guarantees of how your spouse will respond. Even though it may be painful, now your relationship can be built on truth. You can work together for healing and wholeness. It's tempting to put on a victim mentality: Poor me, why did this happen to me? You can also make the choice to rejoice. Your spouse is finally being honest! Now you can work on this together and never let the enemy divide you again!

If you're hiding things, renounce those hidden elements of sin and shame. Today may not be the day. Sometimes you want to vomit all this garbage, and your spouse is devastated. Your prayer should be, "Lord, prepare the way for this confession. Show me the timing for when my spouse is ready to hear what I need to say. Help us to bring transparency, healing, purity and wholeness back into our relationship."

There is such joy in transparency. Our prayer is that each of you will become whole and free, honest and transparent with each other, reaching a depth in your relationship that you've never had before. When we first became great friends, one of the things we loved most is that we could tell each other absolutely everything about ourselves.

The other drew it out, went inside our hearts and explored our views, opinions, passions and desires. One key element in a strong, healthy marriage is to know and understand one another. And for women, there's nothing more romantic than for her husband to pursue her and know her deeply.

The Five Love Languages, by Gary Chapman

We have been tremendously helped by Gary Chapman's book, *The Five Love Languages*[1], in teaching us how to understand each other's language and be a great friend and lover. Judging from the way many married couples communicate (or, rather, fail to communicate), you would think that they did not speak the same language. So often, the problem in troubled marriages is not that spouses don't love each other anymore. Their problem is in communicating their love in ways that are mutually understood and meaningful. In other words, they don't share a common love language.

Over the years, Dr. Gary Chapman has counseled thousands of married couples who are seeking to restore the mutual and affirming love they once knew. Throughout all of his counseling he has found that truly connecting with a loved one came down to one simple fact: You need to know and speak his or her love language. A love language is the way we express our devotion and commitment, and it can be learned or changed to touch the hearts of our partners.

Whether you're a spouse, a parent, or a single, the five love languages are the same:

Words of Affirmation

Receiving Gifts

Quality Time

Acts of Service

Physical Touch

The two of us can't encourage you enough to get your copy of the best seller, *The Five Love Languages* and learn the love language of your spouse.

The Basic Rules

Dear brothers and sisters, be quick to listen, slow to speak, and slow to get angry.
James 1:19

Perhaps the most essential quality for good communication in any relationship, and particularly in a marriage, is to be a good listener.

Before jumping into this thing too deeply, however, a few ground rules are in order.

Be careful to cover each other. Make sure that you both agree that the purpose of your sharing is to promote healing and bring a deeper sense of protection and safety to your marriage.

Resolve together that everything you do and say will come from a posture of love. Agree that your mutual goal is not to fix each other but to love, value and desire each other for who you already are rather than for whom you each hope the other will become.

Look into each other's eyes and say, "You are not my problem, nor are you my answer." This relieves both of you from the burden of carrying expectations you cannot fulfill.

Understand together that becoming vulnerable is an inescapable part of the journey to intimacy. Pledge before each other that neither of you will exploit or take advantage of the other's vulnerability but will instead be sensitive, show respect and provide protection and security.

The very thought of intimacy can be exhilarating for one spouse and bone chilling to the other. Our prayer is that you will pursue one another before a crisis in your marriage demands a choice from either of you that you are unprepared to make. Growing your relationship to the place where you both feel safe to be completely transparent, open and honest with each other will lead you into a level of intimacy that will strengthen your marriage to last a lifetime!

>
> *The very thought of intimacy can be exhilarating for one spouse and bone chilling to the other.*

Heart Revelation: The Tough Questions

Counting all costs, are you committed to truth as a lifestyle in your marriage?

Will you take up the greatest challenge you will ever face by being willing to deepen your level of communication?

Are you willing to embrace personal humility and a willingness to lay down your life for the sake of communication in your relationship?

Do you receive your spouse's deep-felt apologies with forgiveness and without lashing back?

Are you hiding something right now that is affecting your marriage intimacy level?

Do you know your spouse's love language? Are you committed to finding out what best speaks to him or her and then using it to express love?

Heart Transformation: The Truth Established

God loves me extravagantly; He wants to communicate with me. (See First John 4:19-21.)

The enemy has no authority in my life; I am surrendered to Jesus Christ and line myself up with His truth. (See Luke 4:18-19.)

God has an opinion about absolutely everything. I can ask Him, and I will hear His voice. (See Matthew 18:19.)

As I love my spouse deeply I can develop a way to identify with him or her. (See John 5:9-13.)

I will not use conversation to degrade, shame or punish my spouse. (See James. 4:1-7.)

Transparency is the way to intimacy. Even though this is scary, God will bless my commitment in having a face-to-face relationship with my spouse. (See Amos 3:3.)

Our relationship can be built on truth. We can work together for healing and wholeness, through the help of God. (See Psalm 91:1.)

There is tremendous joy in transparency with God, myself and with my spouse.

Prayer

Before we pray together, sometimes the best way to begin to express feelings is to use a journal. Being as honest as possible with God is a safe place to start.

Lord Jesus, I confide in You right now. I want total transparency with You and with my spouse. I yield to Your purifying process for my heart. I confess my sin to You [be specific]. Please give me the right words and the right timing for revealing my heart. I pray that you will prepare both of our hearts for complete honesty. I pray that you will help us to develop a healthy way of expressing our thoughts and emotions to each other. We depend on You to help us to communicate.

Father, I want to thank You for moving powerfully in my life. Where there have been hidden things, I realize that this confession is just the beginning. May Your cleansing be brought into my heart. Deal with me so that I will hear Your voice. I want to be obedient to walk through the process of transparency under the guidance of Your Holy Spirit. Thank You for the wholeness that will take place as a result.

God, I believe for the very best. I pray that we will both be whole and free, honest and transparent with each other and get to a depth in our relationship that we've never had before. Thank You, Jesus.

Sweet Conversation: No One Would Have Known

They lived an average Christian life, and no one would have known. There were secrets between them that held them back from true intimacy with each other, and it took a devastation to start the healing process. Walking by the computer, she turned it on and found conversations taking place in a chat room that made her shake. Her husband was living a double life – meeting women on line, then meeting them in person and committing adultery.

She phoned us and we planned a meeting. It was during this time that they sat on the couch and began to communicate in a transparent way with one another. We encouraged them to face each other, look into each other's eyes and really talk. It was difficult for them, but when he finally looked at her face, he admitted, "I haven't really looked into your eyes for years."

It was the beginning of a journey toward true intimacy and honest communication. It is conversations like this that may be painful, but they save marriages and bring the power of truth into a marriage.

[1]Gary D. Chapman, *The Five Love Languages: How to Express Heartfelt Commitment to Your Mate* (Northfield Publishing, 2004).

4

SELFLESS SURRENDER

We know you want to succeed. But how? Most people think of success as getting all they can, accomplishing all their goals and living a life of ease. A successful life, however, is a satisfied life that is also satisfied in love. That kind of success is the deepest kind of all, and it starts with giving up.

In today's culture, someone who says, "I give up," is written off as a loser; defeated and done. However, this is not the kind of giving up we're talking about. We're talking about selfless surrender, the giving up of one-self for the good of another, which in the eyes of God merits the highest honor. The Bible says, *"Humble yourselves before the Lord, and he will lift you up"* (James 4:10, NIV). God's enablement in becoming best friends and best lovers is available to you, but it requires the great exchange: giving up your life and receiving His! This chapter will allow you to accomplish success in a way you never knew possible: by giving up rights, dying to your own self, and finding the power of a surrendered life.

>
> *God's enablement in becoming best friends and best lovers is available to you, but it requires the great exchange: giving up your life and receiving His!*

Do you want to be counted wise, to build a reputation for wisdom?

Here's what you do: Live well, live wisely, live humbly. It's the way
you live, not the way you talk, that counts.
James 3:13, MSG

Our son Robert loves reading bedtime stories. Recently, after hearing the story of Adam and Eve, he reiterated the premise to one of our
teenagers: "I learned that it's really bad to eat apples!" Man was never
intended to have wisdom within himself; he was to have access through
his spirit to God's wisdom! Satan said, "Grab wisdom for yourself; that
way you don't have to depend on God." After eating the fruit, Adam
and Eve discovered that Satan had lied. Wisdom was not to be found in
the fruit of the Tree of the Knowledge of Good and Evil; it was where it
always had been, in the Tree of Life; that is, in Christ, *"in whom are hid-*
den all the treasures of wisdom and knowledge" (Colossians 2:3, NIV).

When man sinned, not only did he lose access to divine wisdom,
but the divine order in his nature fell into ruin. The Tree of the
Knowledge of Good and Evil inflated his soul powers as well as his
physical appetites! We see this even today. Some people are ruled by
their intellect; others, by their emotions. A strong will manifests in
some while others are dominated by their bodily appetites or physical
drives. None of these was meant to rule – and none is capable of ruling! Thus a great power struggle exists between all of these various
drives and desires as each clamors and claws for dominance. Man ends
up hopelessly at war with himself. The only way out is to be saved, so
that our human spirit is restored to a life-giving relationship with God.

Popular wisdom says that in order to succeed you've got to push
your way to the top. But this is not God's wisdom. God resists the proud
and promotes the humble. It's not surprising that being "happy" is a
great goal for a successful marriage. We've been trained through dating
to find the one who makes us happy! And when that certain someone
stops making us happy, we simply break it off. It's so simple. We con-
clude that there must be someone out there who will be better at making us happy.

Typically, our dating system starts by asking, "Who do I want to choose to spend time with? Someone to whom I'm attracted physically, emotionally, intellectually and spiritually." Most dating relationships are based on finding someone who pleases us. It's all about "me, *me, me!*" Someone who makes me feel good; someone who challenges me. And it works until the relationship brings hurt and disappointment, at which point we simply drop that person. Sound familiar? How many times has it happened to you?

So now we're hurt and rejected, and we go off to find another person! Now our goal is to use that person to help cover up our emotional pain. In other words, we're on the rebound! If we practice this cycle sexually as well, then by the time we get married we are so broken and wounded and our hearts are so ripped to pieces that we have very little to give into our covenant marriage.

Do you think this routine will be forgotten when we get married? No! We all enter marriage with the dream and goal of ultimate happiness. The first time disappointment or difficulty comes along, what is our immediate thought pattern? "I'll get rid of him or her and find someone who will make me happy!" No wonder reestablishing covenant is such an important factor in being best friends and best lovers. Who can you trust to be loyal to you forever?

Being happy is just a side benefit of being married. Marriage is much more about God's calling and purpose. It isn't primarily about our being happy; it's about a kingdom and God's call to us to seek His glory and His purpose. Approaching marriage with this mindset actually results in more personal pleasure and enjoyment in the knowledge that we are accomplishing God's eternal purpose. Believe it or not, that is incredibly fun and leads to an amazingly happy marriage.

So, being self-serving will actually make you unhappy. The sooner you realize that you are to give lavishly and be more concerned about your spouse's needs than your own, the sooner you'll discover the power behind this oxymoronic secret!

Don't be selfish; don't live to make a good impression on others. Be humble, thinking of others as better than yourself. Don't think only about your own affairs, but be interested in others, too, and what they are doing.

Philippians 2:3-4

The Dynamic Duo

If this discussion of humility has prompted you to consider your own attitude and you sense a need for a change, take it to the Lord. You might wish to pray something like this: "God, I've been selfish. I've been using my marriage to make me happy. I've had it all wrong, and I need You to transform my heart."

That's where the change must take place: in your heart. Not in your spouse's heart, but in your heart. It's not your job to change your spouse. Has it ever occurred to you that your spouse's "annoying" behaviors may be a response to your attitude? Perhaps if you change, your spouse will change.

So stop trying to fix your spouse. That "mission" in your life must be terminated immediately. Your goal must be to give life. Imagine what could happen if your spouse starts to do the same? The dynamic turns into the dynamic duo: both of you living for the other, to bless, honor and love unconditionally.

But what if your spouse does not change his or her ways? God is more concerned about your character than about the knowledge you possess or the success you make of your life. The fulfillment and satisfaction you receive from giving generously with humility in your heart will reap rewards both in heaven and on earth!

Personal wholeness fulfills and satisfies, making you ready to be a best friend and a best lover. This may be a huge paradigm shift for you. Instead of constantly praying, "Oh God, please change my spouse! Let him or her see what they're doing to me!" you begin to pray, "God, please change me! Help me to put his or her interests ahead of my own.

In order to have my needs met, I'm going to look to You."

The Stone in Your Shoe

When your spouse has disappointed you or made you angry and you believe you are completely justified in your emotion, think of it as entering into the land of opportunity. These are the times when you can invest largely into being a true best friend. A best friend will feel the hurt, pain, or even betrayal but will choose to forgive deeply from the heart. A true friend will also speak the truth in love: *"An open rebuke is better than hidden love! Wounds from a friend are better than many kisses from an enemy"* (Proverbs 27:5-6).

Harboring bitterness is like having a stone in your shoe. Its sharp edges lay just at the place where your foot presses on it the hardest. You wince and grit your teeth with every step. Bitterness will always hurt you more than the one you're attempting to punish. And multiple stones of bitterness make progress in life nearly impossible.

The smart thing to do would be to take off your shoe, dump out the stones and continue on with new freedom and a smile on your face. Forgiveness is a gift you give yourself! It's easier said than done, however, and it's absolutely vital that you have received forgiveness before you try to extend forgiveness to another. Receive this marvelous gift from God, and then give it away. It's the ultimate test of best friends.

As much as God opposes the proud and gives grace to the humble, the Bible also says "A broken and repentant heart, Oh God, you will not despise" (Psalm 51:17). No one enjoys the thought of being broken. Imagine the uselessness of a smashed vase or a bicycle with a bent frame. However, to be irresistible as a best friend and best lover to your spouse, there is an element of brokenness that you can't ignore! Jesus effectively fulfilled His calling, walked in strength and saved the world from sin – and described Himself as One who was completely dependent on His Father.

We want you to understand true brokenness. It's like a horse submitted to its master. Even the strongest, fastest and most capable horse will be kept in the stable during times of war if it isn't completely broken. A broken horse will be obedient no matter what it sees. Even if it perceives danger, a broken horse will follow the lead of its master in complete trust and obedience. As you follow God in your marriage in brokenness, He can use you in your strengths, your influence, your talents and your wholeness.

Getting to the place of brokenness sometimes takes personal tragedy, but it doesn't have to. Our prayer for you is that you won't waste the painful times in life, but rather run to the Father in times of hardship and rejection. His mercy and grace bring healing and redemption. Even the worst of times can eventually result in an improved you; that is, one humble and broken, prepared for greatness!

Living life in unquestioning obedience to God your Father invites adventure, excitement and reward. The value and effectiveness of your life is only as powerful as the extent to which you follow God with an unyielding heart.

Being broken means dwelling in a state of meekness and strength. Your God-given abilities and talents are valuable to Him and can be used for His ultimate glory as you yield your life in radical submission.

If your marriage contains two stubborn people, each waiting for the other to apologize and, therefore, "lose," you've both got it all wrong. The one who forgives freely, willingly and easily is always victorious.

***

Casting the Stone

I was at Bob's mercy when I sat as his feet and confessed my sin of betrayal. I wanted him so badly, and I wanted forgiveness, yet I knew I deserved nothing but pain and punishment. Working through those months of pain and punishment brought much light to our relationship. My perceived need to perform and to earn him back was actually based in fear, while his punishment of me was an attempt to guarantee it wouldn't happen again. With this dance of fear going on we were unable to enjoy being best friends, even though deep down that's what we both wanted.

Our story could have ended right there: both of us trying to recuperate, trying to survive, but neither of us knowing how to reach beyond our pain and receive a new point of view from the Lord. That's what happens to the majority of people who go through pain, disappointment and betrayal in their marriages.

***

But there's so much more! It is in those places of pain that God wants to step in and give you an entirely new perspective. When the forgiveness runs deep, the friendship becomes transparent communion, a bond that is three-fold, not easily broken. You, your spouse and God knitted together, knowing your need for Him and embracing His presence. That's glory in your relationship!

When there is an issue in your marriage, the wrong must be acknowledged, responsibility accepted and forgiveness sought. Just saying, "I'm sorry," doesn't necessarily indicate that the one asking forgiveness has embraced humility and is acknowledging personal wrong and accepting responsibility. Jesus said that we are to forgive up to seventy times seven wrongs! But forgiveness is not an acknowledgement that what happened was right, or that it doesn't matter. Forgiveness deals with our feelings and our responses to the one who has injured us. It is letting him or her go free...and it is the choice of our will to give it.

Forgiveness finishes an issue. When we forgive, we are saying that we will never mention this again to anyone, ourselves included. We won't resurrect it so we can wallow in self-pity again. Forgiveness is a done deal. With this kind of radical forgiveness, angry feelings against each other quickly subside. And if there's a struggle, follow the advice of Jesus: Begin by blessing your spouse and praying for him or her. The negative feelings will quickly evaporate.

What happens if your spouse won't forgive you? Or what if the offender refuses to take responsibility for his or her actions? The ultimate release for your feelings in painful situations like this is unilateral and unconditional forgiveness, such as Jesus modeled on the cross: *"Father, forgive them, for they do not know what they are doing"* (Luke 23:34, NIV). This releases you from the power of the situation and prevents the intrusion of malice and resentment. This issue no longer threatens your growth, your wholeness and your peace. You are free!

***

It was Valentine's Day, 2003. Two years had passed since that pathetic day when I tried to let Bob know I loved him through presents and balloons just two weeks after confessing my sin of adultery. Robert was now 16 months old. Two of our very close friends, Pam Thum and Stephen Marshall, were in town as guests on *It's a New Day*, as well as two new guests we hadn't met before: Dr. Don and Mary Colbert. Pam and Steve were one of the first couples we told about the adultery and pregnancy, and their intense love and faithful prayers carried us through many long nights and painful days. It was Friday night after a big week, and Mom had cooked an extravagant dinner for all of us in her home.

That Valentine's Day is marked in my heart forever. After dinner, Dr. Don began ministering to all of us. As he was praying for me, he identified acute grief that was locked up deep in my heart. He went on to explain that we all go through grief, but that this was something different. It was the result of extreme loss of something or someone, and this grief was locked inside.

Everyone was quiet as I looked around the room. I then proceeded to tell the story of what had happened just two short years before. My grief was locked in because I hadn't yet forgiven myself for what took place. I held in the sorrow and pain and kept it close to my heart. On the outside, few people would notice. God knew, however, and I quickly discovered that I was in the middle of yet another divine appointment.

Dr. Don told me that the key to unlocking my grief would be found in changing my belief system. He instructed me to repeat after him: "It is good for me to get rid of this grief. It is good for Bob that I get rid of this grief. God's plan is that I get rid of this grief. I need to get rid of this grief. I want to get rid of this grief." So far, all was going well. I repeated his statements easily – until he got to the last one: "I deserve to get rid of this grief." I couldn't say it. Deep down I still believed I needed to be punished. I didn't deserve to be completely free. God had a different idea. He loved me so much that He had orchestrated this night in this place with these people so that I could be liberated.

We prayed to correct my belief system, and I finally understood from God's perspective that I deserved to get rid of my grief. I finally accepted my place as His daughter who had always been forgiven. I no longer had to hold on to the grief. The next step was to begin to feel my suppressed grief…deeply.

The reason for this is that we try to manage, suppress, subdue and starve painful thoughts by filling our minds with other things. Meanwhile, the memory is festering deep inside and can resurface at any moment. Someone says something or something happens and this festering wound rises up at exactly the wrong time, resulting in out-bursts of rage and anger. We can control such memories for only so long. We all like to control our emotions and express only the ones that are socially acceptable. Phrases like, "I love you," "I don't like that," and "That tastes good," are all fine and good, but deep inside are conflicting feelings. On this night I was asked to feel every one of them. I needed to go as deep as I could.

This process was not to bring up or glorify ugly emotions, but to bring the hidden pain to the surface. God wants to go to the deep crevices of our hearts and love us in those places. It is our deepest wounds and hurts that He wants to heal by ministering His uncondi-tional love to us. Allowing Jesus to go to these deep or hidden memo-ries brings the healing salve of the Lord to the festering wound. Paul wrote in Ephesians 3:18: "*And may you have the power to understand, as all God's people should, how wide, how long, how high, and how deep his love really is.*" He wants to go deep with His love, but we don't think we deserve this. We think, "I blew it. I messed up. I need to earn it." That's a wrong belief system, and it prevents us from letting God remove the hooks in our life that trigger anger, bitterness and self-pity.

Dr. Don asked me to remember the hard things, like how it felt to tell Bob and to tell the kids and how it felt to know that I had completely betrayed them and had no way to turn back the clock. As I thought on these things, I began to feel the reality of what I had done as never before. My feelings of regret turned into wailing. For the first time, I saw the full devastation of my sin and grieved over it. I saw my sin the way God did, and then let it go. As I grieved, and allowed Jesus to love me in each painful thought or memory, I released it out of my system. To say this was intense would be an understatement! The whole process lasted probably an hour. Afterward, there was such a sweet presence of the Lord in the room! I wasn't disqualified. God turned my mourning into dancing! He gave me beauty for ashes.[1]

***

The night after Audrey was so powerfully released from her grief, I experienced a deliverance of my own. As with Audrey's repentance, I had gone through my forgiveness in layers. Incident after incident, thought after thought, I would choose to forgive, hoping that one day the pain and torment would stop.

Once again, the Colberts were God's instruments for bringing healing. As in Audrey's case, the first thing they did was to challenge my belief system. I needed to be reassured of my identity in Christ: who I am in Him and Who He is in me.

Next, we dealt with the forgiveness issue. I knew I had to forgive. I wanted to forgive. It was good for me, it was good for Audrey, and it was good for everybody else. As the Colberts began to pray, they asked me to remember everything and feel it as deeply as possible: every emotion and every thought, even the worst and most unimaginable.

I talk with a lot of other men who have been through the agony of their wives committing adultery. Most of them have never seen their wives in bed with another man. I had formed a picture in my mind, almost like a video, of Audrey with the other guy. Every act she was involved in, I created it in my own mind down to the last detail: where they were, what took place, what they said, how they touched. The Bible calls this "vain imagination." Second Corinthians 10:5 tells us to take every thought into captivity to the obedience of Christ. We can become caught up in vain imaginations. Sure, these things are true, they did take place; but these thoughts, these vain imaginations create a reality that affects our bodies. Our physical bodies respond to these imaginary visuals just as if we were seeing them for real right before our eyes.

Dr. Don began praying, and I began to revisit that imagination. I was weeping and crying and letting go and it was all being lifted from me. Jesus had always been there, right in the middle of my pain. I realized that there was nothing left. Surprisingly, I couldn't feel the hurtful memories anymore. I couldn't cry anymore. I thought that was it. Dr. Don clearly knew there was more. He said, "There has got to be something you aren't dealing with."

Then the Holy Spirit brought it to my memory. I had created a visual of the time Audrey had gotten pregnant; their last time together. I had every detail formed in my mind. I already knew where and when, and I visualized the rest in my head. I believed my life would have been all right if that one event had never happened. I had to revisit it. When I forgave that act of adultery it was as if a dam had broken. These trapped deadly emotions were released, and His river of life and love swept over me.

All of a sudden it wasn't just about me. For all this time, my self-righteous attitude had blinded me from seeing the other side. I saw Audrey's hurt and loss for the first time. Compassion for Audrey overwhelmed me and I saw with new eyes how my beautiful bride was violated in such an ugly circumstance. Jesus was asking me the question, as I saw her, "Will you be in agreement with Me and rescue her?"

It was powerful. The poisonous venom of bitterness dropped away from me, and I became whole. We fell into each other's arms and wept. This embrace was like none other. In that significant moment we recaptured untainted and true love. It was freedom such as we had never felt before. After going through this process of radical forgiveness, Audrey instantly felt safe again for the first time in years. There was no more need to perform. Our relationship was at rest.

My unforgiveness and Audrey's grief and inability to forgive herself had restricted us from being the "whole" people God intended us to be. And if we weren't whole, we wouldn't be able to have that "10" marriage for which we longed. Before these deep-seated issues were released in our lives, we were doing all right. We would not have known that we needed prayer for these things. The Lord knew, however; He made us aware so that we were able to repent for holding onto them for so long, and we received cleansing and forgiveness.

None of this is natural; it's all supernatural. Love Audrey as Christ loves the church? I couldn't do it. Not alone. When I connected to the source – Christ – I could begin to love her that way because I saw with new eyes. It really is the life of Christ living through me.[2]

***

Bob and I had had a great marriage before; but since embracing the cross and allowing reconciliation to take place by experiencing supernatural forgiveness, I cannot describe the depth of our friendship. We laugh together, we dream together, we stumble together and we catch each other. We know that our love for each other is unconditional, and our covenant together is secure; no longer are we each other's enemy or problem. We have learned to fight for each other, rather than against each other.

Our friendship is different now. I don't fear Bob, what he will say, or whether he will punish. Instead of performing when fear wants to grip me, I remember that perfect love casts out all fear, and the most loving thing I can do is not to perform, but simply to love. And forgive! Forgiveness is the ultimate gift in any friendship. We will fail each other, we will cause pain, and we will be confronted with pain. Our response is our opportunity to grow and live satisfied.

**

Damaged Beyond Repair

When Adam and Eve sinned in the garden of Eden, man's relationship with God was damaged beyond repair. We could do nothing to undo the sin that we had placed between ourselves and God. But God already had a plan in place to reunite us with Him. His heart has always ached for the days of sweet communion with His people. His original design for mankind to be in harmony and communication with Him and they with each other was now challenged. He knew that it was the sin that brought separation, and He knew the only price for sin is death. So He planned the death of His only Son, Jesus, on the cross to cover for us. He wanted us to be reconciled with Him and knew this was the only way.

Reconciliation is completely dependent on God and His divine nature of grace. God, in His grace, reached out to us through Christ, blotting out our sins, and reconciling us to Himself. This is the most amazing news you will ever hear and understand! We aren't alone, and we don't have to carry the guilt and shame of the past. Will you live a satisfied life, or a life of lack and loneliness? The bottom line for these questions lies in this one: Will you choose to accept the invitation to be reconciled with God?

Salvation restores what was lost. What was lost in the garden was a face-to-face close relationship with God. To reconcile, the penalty of sin must be paid. Sin cannot go unpaid. If so, He would not be a just God. He didn't simply forgive sin and say things were now okay. Jesus actually became sin for us.

This question is so important because reconciliation is totally dependent on God. No one can be reconciled with another person until he or she is reconciled to God. He's the only way. You must choose Him first, before you can proceed to be reconciled to your spouse. You can't be best friends and best lovers apart from God. That's why couples get confused when they both assume that they know how to be reconciled, and it doesn't work!

Out of His immense and inexpressible love for you, God wants to give you new life. He has brought us back to Himself through Christ's death on the cross. It was at this moment that He reconciled the world to Himself, and would no longer have to count people's sins against them. God made Christ, who never sinned, as the offering for our sin, and now we can be made right with God! Through His Son, Jesus Christ, God did everything necessary for us to be reconciled and restored to a right relationship with Him.

Through Jesus, we are recipients of this great promise. In Jesus, God has given us the ability to walk in friendship with Him and live according to His standards. Through the cross, our sins can be cleansed and our idols destroyed. He has put within us a new, responsive heart and enabled us to recognize and obey His voice.

The Reconciliation of the Cross

At the heart of our problem with reconciliation is alienation. Unresolved conflict will separate and divide us, leaving us feeling lonely and isolated. Left alone, these feelings will grow and fester until we begin to think that the whole world is against us. At that point, despair and hopelessness are not far away. Looking at our present circumstances we see no redeeming hope, and fear grips our hearts. Feeling alone and defenseless, we lash out at each other, each blaming the other for the problems and for the impasse, and yelling at the other person to change. Instead of recognizing our share of responsibility for the problem, we simply become more deeply entrenched in our own self-serving point of view. Our stubbornness becomes a grudge, which grows into bitterness and then resentment. With these forces in control, we end up doing and saying things we would never before have believed possible, which only makes the problem worse. And all of this stems from alienation.

Alienation is a primary result of man's original rebellion against God. Our alienation from God causes us to become alienated from others as well as from ourselves. Alienation in all its forms is second nature to our fallen nature, while reconciliation is wholly dependant on God and His divine nature of grace. For this reason, if we are to become effective reconcilers in our own lives and relationships, not to mention in our ministry of reconciling others to God, we must understand God's method of restoring stressed and broken relationships. It is the cross of Christ.

> *For God in all his fullness was pleased to live in Christ, and by him God reconciled everything to himself. He made peace with everything in heaven and on earth by means of his blood on the cross. This includes you who were once so far away from God. You were his enemies, separated from him by your evil thoughts and actions, yet now he has brought you back as his friends. He has done this through his death on the cross in his own human body. As a result, he has brought you into the very presence of God, and you are holy and blameless as you stand before him without a single fault.*
> Colossians 1:19-22

The cross of Christ is the effective means of all reconciliation, not only in the relationship between God and the human race, but in all relationships. In other words, the cross is the answer to all the various forms of alienation and division caused by sin. Every one of the great biblical words used to describe reconciliation has the theme of restoring something back to its original design or purpose. *Redemption* means buying back someone who was sold into slavery; *regeneration* means restoring life to something that has lost its life or usefulness; *salvation* carries the sense of salvage, of rescuing something from potential destruction.

The cross of Christ remains the only divine resource for ultimate reconciliation of all relationships. It not only reconciles humanity to God, but also each of us to one another. And it also reconciles us to ourselves, taking our inner conflicts and making us whole, undivided and fully integrated people again. The cross of Christ is the divine arbiter in all disputes. It reaches as far as sin has gone and restores all that sin has damaged. The cross is where the eternal, redeeming, measureless love of God is outpoured into our lives. And it is at the cross that we experience the transforming effect of love freely given. There is a resource of supernatural love at the cross so great that it knows no bounds and can restore to life human love that has been hurt to the very point of death.

The cross of Christ is the ultimate revelation of the nature and character of God. It gives vivid witness to the mercy and faithfulness of God in the midst of all the tragedy, distress, pain, hurt and iniquity of the fallen world we live in. God is good all the time. Once we have that truth established in our hearts, we can trust Him without fear, doubt or reservation.

In the New Testament, the word *reconciliation* is used to describe the total result of Jesus Christ's life and death that has permanently changed the relationship between God and mankind by changing their attitudes toward each other. The aim of reconciliation, therefore, is the restoration of righteousness. Because we use the word *justification* to describe the process of becoming righteous, we tend to think of righteousness as a legal term when in fact it is a relational term. Righteousness means to be rightly related. To be righteous before God is to be in right relationship with Him. And relationship has to do with reconciliation.

>
> God is good all the time. Once we have that truth established in our hearts, we can trust Him without fear, doubt or reservation.

***

Attitude Check

Reconciliation involves a change of attitude because attitudes are all important in relationships. In the Meisner home, attitudes rule, whether mine toward Audrey, hers toward me, ours toward the children or theirs toward us as parents. Attitudes carry the power to determine in this moment whether or not we will have a right relationship; whether there will be harmony or discord.

Attitudes differ according to our beliefs. Beliefs are largely cognitive; that is, they affect the way we think about issues, they help form our values and directly relate to our relationships with each other. We generally don't act according to our beliefs, but we do act in accordance with our attitudes. In other words, our behavior reveals our attitude regardless of what we say. For example, there was a time when I believed that I loved my wife, but my actions didn't demonstrate that love. My attitude was one of anger, sorrow and control. I allowed myself to be ruled by my emotions and vain imaginations that were directly affecting my attitudes and thereby preventing the healing or reconciliation process.

In my journey toward healing and reconciliation with Audrey, I began to see and understand more fully the work of the cross in my life. I discovered that I was completely incapable of standing on my own. Everything I had believed to be true was being challenged. My capacity to love was nearly drained. My attitude toward everything that was happening in my life was leading me to the conclusion that we had "irreconcilable differences." Left unchecked, my attitude would have made reconciliation with Audrey impossible. I needed a new point of view.

My viewpoint changed the more I understood the cross and what Christ did for me there. Because of Christ's death, God's attitude toward us changed from wrath to blessing. Christ's death changed us from hostile rebels to loving sons and daughters of God. Please don't misunderstand me; God's feelings toward us have never changed. His disposition toward His fallen creation has always been that of unconditional, unchanging, infinite love. But God's attitude toward sin must always be holy wrath. Sin is an offense which God cannot overlook and remain a holy God.

This is why our reconciliation to God necessitated atonement. Atonement is the covering of sin by something that robs sin of its power to permanently disrupt our relationship with God. The sin covering that made our reconciliation possible is the blood of Christ. Atonement also involves judgment. God's judgment of sin fell on the only One who could bear it: the Man Christ Jesus, our Representative and our Substitute. God reached into a sin-sick world with Jesus to recapture our hearts with His love. In Jesus, the Father found a foothold within humanity to make a change of heart possible.

What am I saying in this? Simply this: My feelings for Audrey have never changed; but I went through a time after her confession of adultery when I had a real attitude problem, becoming very judgmental with a strong urge to punish. Here's the bottom line: How do we move from this place of alienation to one of reconciliation? How do we translate the reconciling power of the cross into our everyday lives and relationships?

We cannot do it in our own strength. In spite of our best efforts, our own human or natural love is inadequate. Faced with major relational strife, I became instantly bankrupt of my own resources of love. I discovered that there was only one place I could turn: the life of Christ in me through the Holy Spirit.

I myself no longer live, but Christ lives in me. So I live my life in this earthly body by trusting in the Son of God, who loved me and gave himself for me.
Galatians 2:20

Christ in me; that was the key. And it is the key for you too: Christ in you.

***

Your Private Sin

There really is no such thing as a "private" sin. Even if no one knows about your sin except you and God, it will still affect those around you because it will change the way you relate to them. Everything you do, whether good or bad, affects your spouse and your children in some way. That is why we were so careful about the way we told our children about the adultery and how we were staying together as a family no matter what happened.

Humility and brokenness are key elements in being irresistible in marriage. However, just like anything else, the enemy has a counterfeit ready for the taking. Imagine an extremely humble spouse. Is it an image of someone with his head hung low, at his or her spouse's every beck and call, ready for a beating at any given moment? That image portrays someone who is simply pathetic – someone who does not know his or her worth in God. Pathetic has absolutely nothing to do with humility!

False humility is actually hidden pride. This may be a mind-bender, but pride sometimes disguises itself as humility! This occurs when someone has the behavior of humility but a heart full of pride, judgment and self-righteousness. True humility can be confident and relentless. Moses actually describes himself as the most humble man on earth. Yes, that's his self-description! (See Numbers 12:3.) He knew his own heart, one that desperately knew its need for God, and was not ashamed to proclaim it!

Being humble is the essence of Who Jesus was. He never ate, walked or breathed without knowing it was the will of His Father. There was no pride in Him, which means no jealousy, impatience, self-importance or selfish ambition.

Our lessons in humility have been long-lasting, deep and, most of the time, private. We recognize the fruit of pride rising up in us almost daily, so we've learned to yearn for humility in hopes of making the battle over pride effortless! Our sojourn continues.

Our prayer for you is that you would know humility and embrace it. As you humble yourself and seek the Holy Spirit's conviction concerning how God longs to heal your heart from pride, you will be exempt from hard hits in life, simply because your own choices will protect you. A heart that knows humility is a heart that is satisfied.

Considering others more important than yourself and being sensitive to others' needs, feelings and desires sets you up as a servant in life. There are two kinds of people in this world: those who serve, and those who wait to be served. The first is the life of reward, fulfillment and discovering true purpose. It's not a matter of changing your behavior; it's a matter of letting God transform your heart.

> *Your attitude should be the same that Christ Jesus had. Though He was God, he did not demand and cling to his rights as God. He made himself nothing; he took the humble position of a slave and appeared in human form. And in human form he obediently humbled himself even further by dying a criminal's death on a cross.*
> Philippians 2:5-8

Conviction from the Holy Spirit is a beautiful thing. For us, it's like an "aaaaahhh" moment when we see ourselves from God's view…a hidden sin that we hadn't seen before, a revelation that reveals a clean-up needed in our hearts. We love days when we are able to repent and receive forgiveness and cleansing, for we know it's just another step to the great exchange: *"not my life that I'm living, but Christ living in me."* Our satisfied heart is forgiven, and is able to be generous in forgiveness.

Heart Revelation: The Tough Questions

As I consider humility, what rules my heart? A powerful intellect? Strong emotions? A masterful will? Or is it my bodily appetites or physical drives?

Did I give my heart to many people before getting married? How has this affected my marriage?

Do I consider my spouse more important than myself? Do I put his or her needs before my own?

Am I a broken one, completely submitted to my Father's will?

Am I willing to forgive, even if my spouse won't apologize or repent?

Why is forgiving one who has failed me so important to our personal restoration?

Am I holding on to grief because of the stupid and selfish mistakes of my past?

Have I tried to reconcile with my spouse apart from God?

Are there specific instances in my life where I need to repent of pride in a particular relationship and ask God for wisdom and humility?

Do I consider others more important than myself?

Do I serve, or do I wait to be served?

Do I tend to follow logic more often than God's leading?

Do I go to God when I'm in pain, in search of a new point of view?

Heart Transformation: The Truth Established

When my spouse disappoints me, I enter into the land of opportunity to invest God's glory into our relationship! (See Matthew 6:33.)

Forgiveness is a gift I give to myself! (See Matthew 6:14.)

God is not holding my sins against me; He's not mad at me. (See Second Corinthians 5:19.)

God is good all the time. Once I have that truth established in my heart, I can trust Him without fear, doubt or reservation. (See Second Timothy 1:7.)

With God all things are possible! (See Matthew 9:26; Proverbs 3:5-6.)

A heart that knows true humility is a heart that is satisfied. (See Mark 10:45.)

Prayer

Father in heaven, I want to live a life of humility and brokenness. I want to be reconciled with You, so that I can be reconciled with others.

I understand what You have already done for me, and I truly know that I am accepted as Your friend. As I begin to pray, I am assured that You have seen every single tear that I have cried. You understand a broken heart and long to reach me with Your accepting love. Everyone in the Bible who received a miracle had to take a step of faith. As I pray, I believe.

I receive what You said: You're not holding my sin against me, and You're waiting for me to come to You and "sup" with You…You want us to hang out, to be together, to be at home in each other. That's what Christ in me means.

I want to have peace. I want my heart to be at rest, because I know that's when sweet fellowship with Jesus starts. The thing that is separating me from You, that bitterness toward my spouse, that pride that keeps me demanding my own way, I get rid of it today.

I'm sorry for thinking You're disappointed in me, and that I have no right to talk to You. Your eyes are on me, waiting for me, wanting fellowship with me, wanting to heal me and wanting to make me a whole person, one who is overflowing with Your love and life. I receive Your grace and enablement to forgive today, and begin life new. I need You so much, and am so thankful for Your love.

Selfless Surrender: She Didn't Intend to Forgive Him

I, Audrey, read a letter that had been lost in piles of paperwork. I had first opened it a couple of months before and begun praying for the woman who had written, but I had never responded to her letter. This particular morning I found myself drawn to just pick up that phone and call this woman whom I had never met.

Her husband had recently confessed to an addiction to pornography, to visiting strip-clubs as well as to an affair. Her small town restricted her from reaching out to friends, in fear of being part of the gossip circles. When she confronted her husband, she had planned to inform him that she was leaving the marriage.

But when she opened her mouth, all she could say was expressions of her love, commitment and forgiveness to him, and that she had been praying for their marriage. She was surprised at her own words, particularly since her original intention had been to leave. He agreed to stay in the marriage and get help. Unfortunately, there was no help to be found. She questioned her commitment to him, yet deep down knew that it was based on God's truth.

During a time of silence in the phone call, I softly spoke out: "You are so beautiful." The silence was broken with quiet weeping, and then sweet ministry. I knew that those words were from her Father in heaven. She received her Father's love and identity. Faith rose up in both of us for complete restoration.

Seizing the opportunity, she is investing forgiveness into her marriage, and the healing she is receiving amid the pain will be used for God's glory one day. They will join the ranks of helping others, and seeing miracles take place as they share pain, struggles and triumph. We're standing in faith!

[1] Bob and Audrey Meisner, with Stephen W. Nance, *Marriage Under Cover: Thriving in a Culture of Quiet Desperation* (Huntsville, AL: Milestones Publishers International, 2005), 137-140.

[2] Bob and Audrey Meisner, *Marriage Under Cover*, 140-143.

5

SATISFYING SEX

Most men, when they hear the word intimacy, immediately think of one thing: sex! Women, on the other hand, think of intimacy as relating to another person on a deep emotional and spiritual level. For guys, being intimate is an encounter. For women, however, it is a rendezvous: a candlelight dinner, soft music, quiet romantic conversation while curled up on the sofa together in front of the fireplace. With such widely disparate conceptions of intimacy, is it any wonder that so many couples never achieve a consistently satisfying level of intimacy in their marriage?

The truth is, God created us as relational beings. He built into us the capacity to enjoy personal relationships. Some, like marriage and family, are very private and exclusive, while others are more public and inclusive, such as a local sports club or church fellowship. Some relationships are intended to be permanent in nature while others are temporary associations. The proper level of intimacy in any relationship depends on the nature, depth and degree of permanence of the relationship. Satisfaction in any relationship is directly related to the degree to which the appropriate level of intimacy is achieved and maintained.

What is intimacy, anyway? Interestingly enough, sex does not figure into any of the formal definitions of the word. Intimacy has to do with our deepest nature – the person we really are inside. It has to do with close contact and thorough familiarity with a subject or a person.

Intimacy can be defined as "a warm friendship developing through long association."[1] In other words, intimacy is all about relationship. There is nothing of the quick encounter about it. Sex between a husband and wife can certainly be intimate in the truest sense of the word, but full intimacy transcends and encompasses much more than just the sex act.

God intended marriage to be the most intimate of all relationships, so close that a husband and wife become "one flesh" (Genesis 2:24). The biggest challenge in reaching a consistently satisfying level of marital intimacy lies in the fact that we all enter marriage with our own ideas of what constitutes intimacy, and our ideas often clash with those of our spouse. We also all differ in our ability to share the deep matters and issues of our heart. Our ability to share has much to do with our own individual backgrounds: the models of intimacy we were exposed to as well as the wounds that we all have and that we guard so carefully. If these differences of perspective on intimacy are not understood or given room for expression, the end result will be a marriage filled with tension and contention, clash and conflict.

Sexual intimacy is an expression of this "one flesh" union. Two people become one person. This happens when a life is given. The price for true sexual union is the giving of our life to and for our spouse. Our sitcoms and modern music (and much of our modern culture, for that matter) tell our young people that sex is recreation; something we give away and participate in as flippantly as sharing a soda. Sadly, for many of us, when we get married and want to give our heart to our covenant partner, our heart is in so many pieces and has been so many places that it's virtually impossible to enjoy precious and pure intimacy. We have totally lost the precious ability of becoming one physically with our spouse because we have already given ourselves to others along the way.

If this scenario describes you, there is a remedy in the finished work of the cross of Jesus Christ. His healing can reach into your past and His forgiveness can cleanse you as you repent of your sins. After repenting, it's important to ask God to direct your heart and spirit to

your spouse alone. After becoming one with other people, your h
and spirit are confused and are not able to give in wholeness to yo
spouse. Some have even admitted that they can be in bed with their
spouse and, because of an unhealed past, sense the power of the memory of being sexual with someone else. (Read more in First
Corinthians 6:12-20.)

The prayer of breaking the ties between you and the other people
you were sexually involved with clears your heart to be made one
with the spouse with whom you are in a covenant relationship. The
Bible says:

*For I am about to do a brand-new thing. See, I have already begun!
Do you not see it? I will make a pathway through the wilderness for
my people to come home. I will create rivers for them in the desert!*
Isaiah 43:19

Although sex is only part of full marital intimacy, most couples with
intimacy problems identify sex as the primary culprit. Usually this is due
to a combination of misinformation
and imbalanced and unrealistic expectations. Much of the misinformation is
due to our society's holding up false and
misleading standards of beauty and of
what makes a person sexy and desirable. This misinformation in turn feeds
unrealistic sexual expectations. The
end result is that both partners feel
inadequate, unfulfilled and unsatisfied.

Best lovers are not necessarily a
young, energetic combination of
Barbie and Ken. What makes a man

*It's time to get honest
with a dark and dirty
secret: the quality of
our thought life
regarding sex deter-
mines the level of
satisfaction in our
sex life far more than
does the condition of
our body.*

manly and a woman desirable is relative, depending on where you are,
at what time, and with whom. Today, more than at any other time in

being deluged with media images that "help" us to ...pposedly masculine and feminine. What a danger to ...n stereotyping instead of God's truth! Perfect bodies ...tee perfect sex. Far from it. The ingredients for a healthy and satisfying sex life do not begin with the body, but with the mind. It's time to get honest with a dark and dirty secret: the quality of our thought life regarding sex determines the level of satisfaction in our sex life far more than does the condition of our body.

**

During my time of healing and restoration after committing adultery I discovered that all my life I have had a warped understanding of the joy in sex. It's not because I asked for it; I've just always tended to think that sex had to be really naughty or dirty to be really good. It would be easy to blame this perception on so many things: the media, past generational sins, lack of protection. But I don't want to assign blame. I'd rather own up to the fact that I've got a wrong concept, repent and ask God for His truth in the matter! I'm not interested in behavioral change as much as in heart transformation. Behavioral change affects only the externals; heart transformation gets to the root of the matter.

If you had asked me ten years ago whether I would ever write a book, I would have answered with complete confidence, "Absolutely!" It would be about intimacy with Jesus. Since I was a little girl my passion has always been to be so close to the Lord that there would be no blocks and no intimidations, just beautiful free relationship. I love to wake up in the morning with Him on my mind and walk and talk with Him all day long. Jesus is my best Friend. He has never left me and His love has never failed me. I love Him passionately.

Well, a couple of years ago I did write a book, but it was nothing like the one I had dreamed of. In fact, Bob and I wrote it together. *Marriage Under Cover* relates the story of our redemption, healing and restoration after my sin of adultery. Does that make any sense? How could a girl who loves Jesus as much as I do become an adulteress?

The simple answer: *"Pride goes before destruction, and haughtiness before a fall"* (Proverbs 16:18). That's why I now love and embrace humility every chance I get. Humility is our protection against sin; it helps us to recognize and understand our deep, inherent need for God every day. But I almost lost everything dear and precious to me before I learned that lesson.

Pride told me that I didn't need boundaries with guys like other girls did. My marriage was strong and protected. Pride said that I could enjoy a little attention on the side because I could control my thoughts and urges and nothing would ever come of it. Pride nearly destroyed me.

The enemy feeds our strength with flattery. Once we embrace pride he enters through the back door to rob, kill and destroy. Sometimes our greatest strengths are also the areas in which we are most vulnerable. Our only sure protection is to be passionately surrendered to Christ, humbly acknowledging that any and every strength we have is because of His Holy Spirit in us. As the Lord said to Paul, *"My gracious favor is all you need. My power works best in your weakness"* (Second Corinthians 12:9). Grace that brings power comes in weakness. It takes weakness to get the grace that makes us strong.

So this weakness, my thinking that sex had to be "naughty" to be good, had been in the back of my mind our entire married life. No problem, really. Bob and I enjoyed great times of intimacy and never fought over sexual issues. We seemed to be perfectly happy and satisfied. Meanwhile, I developed scenarios of "naughty" sex that I would give in to in order to reach a climax. I never got close to another man, never watched porn and never did anything else improper. I didn't think my dark and dirty little secret was harmful, so I never told Bob about it.

Then a relationship developed in which an individual pursued me relentlessly and triggered my hidden secrets. My thoughts gave birth to sin and before long I plunged headlong into an adulterous affair.

When did my downward spiral toward sin begin? Long before I got married. The Song of Solomon speaks of love that is awakened before its time. "Love" awakened me as a young teenager and sin developed a stronghold in my mind. I craved attention from guys and loved the thought that I was attractive. The neighborhood boys took advantage of me and lies were written on my heart.

One of these lies told me that in order to get attention I had to let myself be used by guys. I wanted to feel beautiful and desirable. I found out that I had to give myself in kissing and fondling to fill my need for love and attention. I began to enjoy the attention, as well as the touching. I'm not talking about intercourse, for my parents taught me clearly about morality and values. And I had the full unconditional love of my earthly father and enjoyed his love, attention and acceptance. But these lies that were written on my heart began to identify me, and I began to think, "This is who I am. This is my weakness, and it is something I will have to resist the rest of my life."

I took this lie with me into my marriage. Even after marrying Bob, a committed Christian man, and helping others in ministry, this sin still had a powerful hold on me – but I had not yet seen the full fruit of its power. I thought the problem would go away as soon as I was married and I could enjoy pure pleasure with my husband; instead, I introduced the naughty scenarios into my thought life.

This is not just my dark, dirty secret; women and men everywhere struggle with the same thing. How do I know? Because wherever I go and share this part of my story I get an overwhelming response from men and women alike acknowledging similar struggles. My experience has convinced me that this is a virtually universal problem.

It's also a problem that the Bible addresses. Let me paraphrase Ezekiel 23.

There were two sisters who became prostitutes in Egypt. As young girls they allowed themselves to be fondled and caressed. The older one lusted after other lovers instead of her husband, and she gave her love to the Assyrians, her neighbors. They were all attractive young men, dressed in handsome uniforms and dashing about on their horses. She prostituted herself with the desirable men, worshipping their idols.

They stripped her and killed her and took her children as slaves. She was known as the sinner who got what she deserved.

The problem was that when she left Egypt, she did not leave her spirit of prostitution behind. Then the Egyptians satisfied their lusts with her and robbed her of her virginity. The younger sister did the same thing. She even fell in love with pictures that were painted on a wall and longed to give herself to these pictures. (Sounds like ancient-day pornography!)

When I read this story, revelation came. I had never left my attitude of prostitution. Prostitution is a job, payment for service rendered, another "thing required of me." Even though Bob and I enjoyed our intimate life together for all of these years, there are times when I have allowed this task-driven attitude to infiltrate our marriage and punish the wonderful man that I love without his even knowing about it. In our Christian walk we have been delivered from slavery. We are no longer slaves to sin, but are sons and daughters of the King. I repented for taking this slave mentality into our marriage instead of enjoying the pure pleasure of intimacy without earning it or having to deserve it. Making love is an expression of love that carries no manipulation, no control, no unrealistic expectations and no fear.

So now we know what not to think about during sex! If our thoughts and heart are not on our spouse, then we aren't really with our spouse. Such thoughts are dangerous and they are robbing married women and men everywhere of a pure, satisfying sex life.

The Porn Problem

There is another dark and dirty secret going around that is devastating more marriages and destroying trust and intimacy between spouses more than perhaps any other force in our society. It is not so much a secret anymore, though. Pornography has always been around, but it has multiplied exponentially since the advent of the Internet. I have seen too many people hurt by pornography; too many lives destroyed. Porn is the secret sin that so many carry, seemingly with no consequences unless they are found out. The damage of pornography begins the moment our eye gate opens the door to our heart. It is almost impossible to steer clear of, and pornographic images are readily available even when we're not looking for them.

As seekers of truth and pure pleasure, we are wise to be aware of what the enemy is doing and aggressively avoid pornography at all costs. For those who already have such images planted in their minds, and which become part of their thoughts during intimacy with their spouses, it is a matter of heart transformation. If pornography is something that you struggle with, take action now! Don't delay another moment! Your intimacy with your spouse will never be what it could and should be until you deal with this issue! Instead of simply trying to resist the temptation, ask God to plant these truths in your heart:

Pornography is destructive.

Pornography will never bring fulfillment.

Pornography will never be satisfied and will always demand more and more.

Pornography is a trap of the enemy designed to destroy your relationships.

You can be free from all the past involving pornography.

Your mind can be cleansed!

Only God can break the bondage of pornography.

Bring the lie to light! Often when we are speaking at marriage conferences, Bob will announce that he can determine anyone's sin that they struggle with the most. It's scary! He asks for volunteers and I watch everyone's face turn white. Is he really going to tell me the sin I struggle with most? He then says, "It's the sin you love the most."

Truth be told, all of us have some sin or sins that we love because we believe we see personal benefit that makes the price worth paying. What a deception! Whether it is unforgiveness, lust, greed, gluttony, jealousy, hatred or whatever, there's a part in each of us that desires the sin, and it is those desires that God wants to transform in our hearts.

Imagine desiring everything that's perfect, right and pure! Talk about effortless victory! Talk about mature growth! Talk about abundant fruitfulness and fulfilled potential! That's finding pleasure and satisfaction in life, and with your spouse that means being best friends and best lovers.

***

Give and Take

As with friendship, in order to have a good lover you must learn to be a good lover! Your love life as a couple will be as unique and original as your friendship. It will be personal to you and will contain qualities that are unlike those of any other couple. Custom-made sex! How about that?

In the same light, your particular problems in your sex life as a couple also will be unique to you. Problems with sexual intimacy have driven couples apart time and time again. Sometimes the problems are emotional: depression, anxiety, fear, resentment, jealousy, low self-esteem, body shame, guilt and so on. Sometimes they are physical: sickness, handicaps, pain during sex, hormonal imbalances, fatigue, common infections and the effects of aging. And sometimes the problems are spiritual: secret sin, past sexual abuse, bitterness, an unforgiving spirit and rebellion. Time and time again, couples share about the walls that come up whenever it's time for physical intimacy. What can you do?

> *As with friendship, in order to have a good lover you must learn to be a good lover! Your love life as a couple will be as unique and original as your friendship.*

Above all, strive to be patient and sensitive with each other. Pray together. Don't be bashful about taking your sex problems to God. After all, He created sex! And He knows just what to do to help both of you find release into the most fulfilling life of intimacy you could ever imagine!

What Did You Expect?

Imagine a rendezvous with your spouse at a great coffee place. You order your drink, sit down on the couch by the fire and enjoy effortless and enjoyable conversation. During your time together there is laughter, there are serious moments, there are quiet moments, and there are loud moments! If you did the same thing again the next day, same two people, same place, same time, your experience would be altogether unique! You may order different drinks, you may be in a different mood and frame of mind, and you may connect at a deeper level. The next day, altogether different again! Something funny may have happened that gets both of you on a roll of fun and light-hearted conversation! You will never have the exact same experience twice.

In this same way, every encounter that you experience together sexually will be different. Different words, different expressions, different moods, different places, different times. It's the same two people doing the same thing, but no two times will ever be the same! Sometimes you laugh your way through it, you may cry your way, and sometimes you pray your way through it! Be loud, be completely quiet, be short, take your time; if it is becoming the same, like a routine, it's time to spice up the creativity. That will look different for every couple, but making your sexual intimacy a priority will be very rewarding! We like to say, "Change is inevitable; growth is optional." The two of you will change, your bodies will change and circumstances will change. The choice is yours whether you will grow in that and embrace new levels and heights to your intimacy. It's never too late to try something adventurous and learn something new.

God has given us all we need for satisfying sex. It's the enemy who says we need a substitute. He'll try to convince you that you lack something. Anyone who uses the Internet knows that pop-up ads are designed to make you second-guess yourself and your relationship, especially with regard to sex. But God intends that the two of you be satisfied together. These times are opportunities in your marriage to be extremely generous and to inhabit God's glory!

***

Where's the Drive?

About now some of you may be thinking, "What about those of us who love Jesus with all our hearts and want to enjoy the gift of sex with our spouse, but don't have a raging sex drive? What should we be thinking about? How can we get in the mood? How can we get ready?"

These are the very questions that I, Audrey, have asked of God for years. Several months ago a thought came to mind. I was taking time to be quiet before the Lord and worship Him. I thought about His qualities that make Him irresistible to me. One of my favorites is His faithfulness. The Psalms say that faithfulness is God's very character. There is nothing I could do that would make Him leave me or forsake me. I responded to His love with extreme surrender and passion for being with Him.

Several years ago, right after I told Bob about the adultery, our pastor challenged us to pray together every day while looking into each other's eyes. This was a new concept for us, and at first I felt kind of foolish. It felt like I was praying to Bob and not to God! Our pastor reassured us of the importance of looking deep into each other's eyes, knowing that the Lord dwells in our hearts.

Now, several years later, this has become a daily occurrence for us. We gaze deep into each other's eyes and thank God, repent before God and bless one another. I've also learned that during our intimate times together, it is powerful to gaze into each other's eyes. It's important to have enough lights on so that we can see each other's eyes and make a connection with our hearts. For the eyes are the windows to the heart. You've most likely heard the expression, "when our eyes met…" There can be deep fellowship and communion as eyes lock into each other's hearts. (As an added bonus, even as we age, our eyeballs will always look the same!)

The presence of God never leaves us; not even when we're making love. So, I wondered, what would happen if I took this next concept and began worshipping the Lord while we make love? What if these were the thoughts that consumed me while we were intimate together? I had opportunity that night to give it a chance. As Bob approached me, I began to fill my heart and mind with thoughts of the Lord. As God has been faithful to me, Bob has been loyal and faithful to me too. As Bob touched me, I found myself voicing my love for him. During that entire time, I clearly remember not being able to say anything but the simple words, "I love you."

What happened next was earthshaking. There was a connection that made me believe that something happened in the heavenlies. Love songs talk about fireworks. This experience took me to heights of worship and intensity that I did not know were possible. As I rested after this encounter, I wept. I could not control the emotions that over-came me after such an experience. Could I have just tapped in to the reason God created sex in the first place? Could this be the moments of heavenly connection that are rarely talked about even in our Christian walk?

I realize this could be controversial, but if we are going to tackle what it means to be best lovers, I would venture to say that God has a lot to do with it. If you think the idea of sex as a spiritual act seems a little overboard, it may be time to think again. We have presumed that the best sex involves adventure, risk, radical letting go and extreme passion. From everything I know about being spiritual, our walk with God is all of those things as well!

The enemy always uses a counterfeit, and he's pretty adamant about making sure we don't find out the secret to what heavenly sex really is: an expression of worship, an act of covenant. Since that time, we don't always pray our way through our time together, but there are times that we do! Our marriage relationship is but a shadow of how Jesus loves His church. We are the Bride, the one He longs for, the one He calls beloved.

Obstacles in "The Heat of Things"

Most people don't talk about it, other than to argue or ask for it, and just hope that everything will work itself out. Or else they get frustrated and find a sleazy worldly way to deal with it, hoping to find climax but missing the point of intimacy.

The enemy would love to put fear and doubt in your heart regarding your own abilities as a best lover. Every person will have unique expressions, and it's important for you to know your value in what God made you to be. There are also practical things to know concerning what to think about that can heighten your experience and take the pressure off!

It's easy to think about abstractions: how to do it right, why it isn't going well, getting bored with yourself, wondering what your spouse is thinking, whether or not your spouse is impatient, whether or not your spouse can last. It would be far better to concentrate on sensations, not thoughts. Women especially get so caught up in their thoughts that they forget to enjoy their bodies!

It could be that you fear you won't have an orgasm, even though you are aroused, and so you don't want to get into the hassle of trying. Thus, you repress your sexual response.

Another fear may be that you are asking too much and seeming demanding of your spouse. Or your spouse may be trying so hard to please you, concentrating on your pleasure, that you feel so much pressure to perform that you fear you won't be able to! Also, your thought patterns can influence your concentration. If you think, "I'll never do this right," or, "I have work to do," these can work against you.

If there is conflict or anger in your marriage, it is difficult to enjoy union with your bodies. Being best friends and being transparent with each other are tremendous benefits to your sexual enjoyment.

When there has been a wrong concept regarding sexual intimacy, such as parents saying it's "bad," or abuse has forced upon you wrong concepts of enjoyment, guilt about having sex can set in, so you can't let yourself really enjoy it.

It's very helpful to "be in the moment" and focus on sensations, feelings and intensity rather than worry about the anticipated end result.

Reduce the pressure you put on yourself. Take the time to have loving thoughts toward your spouse. Work to create an atmosphere that encourages peace and enjoyment. You will notice immediate benefits.

Transparent conversation about your expectations of each other as well as your struggles and challenges brings warmth and acceptance into your sexual relationship. Make it a priority to understand your spouse, who is different from you in sex drive, energy level and expression. And be patient; it will take a lifetime for you to know each other in every intimate detail. Overcoming obstacles brings you closer to each other. Practicing humility and unconditional love as you pass through life's storms together will bring increasing tenderness into your relationship.

Sex that satisfies is a reward of intimacy. Satisfaction is different for every single person. This is so important to remember! Being best lovers does not mean you have to have crazy sex every chance you get! More and more our society takes its sexual cues from Hollywood and its often warped and fantasized views of sex. If you fill your mind with those ideas and carry them into your bedroom, your sex life will never become what it could be because you are caught up in fantasy. Fantasy is not founded on truth!

Are You Bored with Your Spouse?

If your life together seems endlessly humdrum, take time together to think back on the last time you did something enjoyable together. What was it? Discuss how you could recapture that same sense of pleasure and satisfaction and start simply enjoying each other again. If you are not satisfied in your love life, you must realize that some dimension of truth has not been established in your heart. Somewhere you are believing a lie. The enemy ultimately wants you to be ineffective and unproductive. If you become frustrated in your marriage, your heart will close up and you will become less effective and productive and begin living for yourself rather than for your spouse.

Marriage is the closest physical example we have to our relationship with God. We are the Bride of Christ! In Him, we are satisfied. The same should be true with our husband or wife; we should sense no lack. That's not to say that life will always seem wonderful and circumstances won't get challenging with hardships, but in all these things, we are not alone! We have everything when we have Him.

Maybe it's time to stop taking life so seriously. Flirting is fun for us. It always has been! We love to be playful in an alluring way, knowing that we're capturing each other's attention and admiration.

I remember seasons in our marriage where I flirted too much with other men. It wasn't sexual, but I knew I was captivating them, and I enjoyed it. Much of the road to adultery in my case was a result of flirtatious behavior. I loved being good at it and getting what I wanted. It almost made me physically sick to type out that sentence. What a disgusting and selfish way to walk down the road of destruction!

I'll never say I'm immune from flirting again, because that would be an arrogant way to slip into pride. But ever since I participated in adultery, I see the whole idea of flirting with other men to be disgusting. I'm fully aware of the consequences of sin and the pain that takes place when I participate with it!

But there's something more powerful than fear, and that is love. Since our restoration in our marriage, my love for Bob is so deep, so intimate; I am completely satisfied in our life together. I don't find myself fantasizing or dreaming of something better. Is this because I'm so good? So pure? No. It's because I am loved so deeply that I don't want any substitute. It's this love from God that fulfills me, and Bob's love for me holds me in protection.

I still flirt. I think it's important to flirt. In fact, Bob and I are pretty good at it, and it makes us smile and communicate love and security to each other in a very spontaneous way. Being playful and alluring at the same time is just another way of being best friends and best lovers.

evelation: The Tough Questions

你 you been able to receive God's point of view for your love life together?

How will you be generous in giving to your spouse sexually?

What are the obstacles that have kept you from a great love life?

Have you struggled with the idea that God made your body and its potential for sexual pleasure? If so, in what way have you struggled?

Have you fantasized about others while being with your spouse?

Has your life been affected by your own or other people's inappropriate sexual activities? Are you able to forgive those who have sinned against you in this way?

Do you know someone who can help to encourage you to stay pure when faced with temptation of pornography?

Do you need to discuss your fears, your frustrations and your dreams for your sexual life together and communicate about hiding or pretending with your spouse?

What goals do you believe God wants you to have in your love life together?

Heart Transformation: The Truth Established

I am totally and completely loved. (See First John 4:10.)

As I am loved, the fear and need to perform is removed. (See First John 4:18.)

My spouse is the one with whom I am in covenant and is therefore the most anointed to satisfy me in every way, including sexually. (See Mark 10:8-9.)

I have everything it takes to give to my spouse sexually, to be extremely satisfied and to be content. (See John 20:22-23.)

I invite God into our intimate relationship, asking for His guidance and wisdom. This is not something we do apart from Him. (See Mark 10:9.)

I will give to my spouse out of abundant love. I am at rest and not striving. (See Isaiah 26:3.)

Great sex does not always equal earth-shaking climax every time, morning noon and night! (See Hebrews 13:4.)

Our private life is one in which we honor each other and do not make jokes about what's personal to one another other while in public. We value this extremely intimate and personal expression. (See First Timothy 5:13.)

I don't have to have a perfect body in order to enjoy sex and give myself with confidence to my spouse. (See Luke 6:38.)

Prayer

Heavenly Father, I just read this chapter and feel convicted by Your Holy Spirit. I've participated with sin, and I'm overcome with guilt and shame. I'm also really scared of being transparent; that if I tell my spouse I'll be rejected and abandoned. I pray that You will step in with Your unconditional love and bring Your peace and reassurance.

First of all, forgive me where I've damaged others and myself through sexual sin. It was a selfish act for which I take full responsibility. I come to You in humility, knowing I need You, so please forgive me for my pride. Lord, I need You. I invite Your presence and truth into my life. I also choose to forgive the person or people who have sinned against me in this way. I ask You today heal my heart and restore me back to the place of opportunity. I want my sexual life to be bathed in truth and full of Your purity and glory. I want Your highest; I want to be the best lover for my spouse.

Thank You for giving me this gift of my spouse. I ask You to give us wisdom regarding our personal life together. I pray that You will give us a plan to overcome the obstacles that are robbing us of being completely intimate.

Thank You, Jesus. I trust You completely. I can't fix anything, but as I give You my life and situation, I know You are powerful and loving, and will be my Friend through this journey. I love You, Lord Jesus.

Satisfying Sex: Healing after Fifty-Two Years

After attending a marriage retreat, an older couple confided in us. They had been married for fifty-two years. Tears were shed as she described how she had been sexually abused by her pastor when she was between the ages of thirteen and eighteen. Her husband struggled with unforgiveness toward her, even though she was the victim. As Bob described his forgiveness for me and how he began seeing me through the eyes of Jesus, not only forgiving me but also rescuing me and loving me, this ministered a whole new level of forgiveness for both of them. After more than fifty years of struggling, God brought a new point of view. They received a deep healing, and could now enjoy intimacy like never before.

[1] *Merriam-Webster's Collegiate Dictionary, Tenth Edition,* (Springfield, MA, Merriam-Webster, Inc., 1993).

6

SCREAMING FREEDOM

We have a vivid memory of a moment of victory in our lives as a couple. After spending an intense weekend with several couples from a church that had hosted us, we listened as reports were given. One young man came up to the front with his wife, took the microphone, silently scanned the audience…then suddenly screamed, "Freedom!" His one word said it all. From being a captive of fear and control, he had experienced profound release. There was cause for celebration!

Satisfaction in love involves many things, but trying to control each other is not one of them. Making it your life's mission to change or fix your partner is not conducive to a healthy, happy marriage! The only thing that lies down that road is misery – for both of you.

Satisfaction in love involves many things, but trying to control each other is not one of them.

Control issues of some kind lie at the heart of virtually every troubled marriage. And sometimes neither partner is even aware of the problem. Consequently, all their efforts to iron out their problems end in frustration and defeat. It is only when those control issues are identified and released that full healing and reconciliation can occur.

Like most other couples, we too had to wrestle with control issues. It wasn't intentional, but both of us were blindly self-serving.

Abstaining from controlling and fixing your spouse is priority number one in becoming irresistible. It was a huge step in our journey to become best friends and best lovers!

In this chapter you will hear from each of us separately, from our own particular perspectives. We'll begin with Audrey.

Controlling Comes Easy: Audrey's Turn

I'm usually a pretty good fixer. My fixing people progress was going pretty well for the first seventeen years of our marriage. I never saw my behavior as controlling; I was merely doing everyone around me favors. Just making their life better for them! In reality, I was carrying a huge load of responsibility that was not mine to carry. And I was tired of carrying it! I kept hoping someone else would pick up the load…or at least the slack!

The truth is, no one can carry what you're holding onto until you let go. After I participated with the sin of adultery, there was no way to fix Bob; too much damage had been done. I knew it was my fault entirely, having handed him the ultimate betrayal after seventeen happy years of marriage.

I would never have dreamed that I would commit adultery. In fact, I felt immune from such a thing. And that was one of my first mistakes! Our marriage was our strongest commodity and our children were the love of our lives. We had dedicated our lives to helping others and bringing the life and truth about Jesus to a hurting world.

That world took on sharp focus in the form of one young man who we were trying to help find his way in life after many hard knocks. Bob and I began investing time, friendship and unconditional love into his heart so that he could understand God's love. Thinking I didn't need the strict boundaries that others did, I became friends with this man, spent time alone with him and presumed I was safe.

His compliments and attention to me fed my selfish pride. I loved the way he adored me and told me how he wished he could find a girl like me. The longer this went on, the more I began to crave his attention. I figured I could play this little game of enjoying him for a while and then go back to my real and true relationship with Bob. As I soon discovered, there's no such thing as a small compromise. Small compromises lead inexorably to large compromises until eventually your whole relationship is compromised. It was at the very beginning of this little game that sin entered my heart, and I gave opportunity for it to grow and fester.

Thinking back on this time in my life, I remember being so confused and, ultimately, selfish. The controlling side of me enjoyed the fact that I could control this game; yet, inevitably there came a pivotal point when the game began to play me. I couldn't control myself any longer. Those compromises grew until I was fully involved in the sin of adultery.

After participating to this degree, I knew it had to stop. I knew I was heading toward ultimate destruction and the loss of everything I knew to be important and loved, so I ended the relationship completely. Then I told Bob everything in hope of restoration and forgiveness. Our book, *Marriage Under Cover*, relates in full the details of this story and our journey to healing and wholeness.

It was during this journey to restoration that I did everything humanly possible to earn back Bob's love. The pain that resulted from my selfish behavior is indescribable, and to this day I can't even begin to fully understand the anguish and torture I caused. Even as I write about it, godly sorrow stirs up the tears and remorse. I never thought I was capable of committing such a horrific deed. But I was, and I am.

Fear gripped my heart: "Bob will never be able to love me again, at least not like he used to. I don't deserve forgiveness and I will live in pain and shame for the rest of my life. Our children will be tainted and affected by my selfish act forever. Our family will never be happy again, and it's all my fault. If I don't earn Bob's trust, he'll punish me and reject me for the remaining years of our marriage."

Fear searches frantically for a fix, which always involves control. Control says, "I must do this myself." Control says, "God is big, yes; but not big enough for this one. I must do everything humanly possible. I would love to trust, but I can't. God isn't answering this one the way I thought He would or could, so I'm going to have to take over. I don't want to do everything myself, but it's the only way things get done on time. I can't waste my life waiting for God to answer my prayer; I have to think of a way to conquer." Do you see all the "I"s? That's a dead giveaway for a control mentality.

God says in His Word that His perfect love casts out all fear (First John 4:18). There is no fear in love.

He invited me to enter into a realm of His love that I had never fully known before. I had to be loved in order to love.

My performance and striving to be the perfect wife and mom were not coming from perfect love. I thought they were. I worked so hard to be perfect; I always expressed love for Bob, even when he rejected me. I remained gentle and non-confrontational and took the punishment I deserved. I assumed I was doing the most loving thing.

I was wrong. If there is fear in love, it's not perfect love. The day God told me to stop changing Bob, He invited me to enter into a realm of His love that I had never fully known before. I had to be loved in order to love. I had to relinquish my performance and trust God relentlessly. My act of letting go was a love gift to God. In fact, when I think of a great present to give God, one that He would absolutely love and cherish, that gift is my trust. Total trust.

I prayed, "I'm so sorry, Lord Jesus, for trying to make this happen. I'm sorry for allowing fear to alter my responses to Bob. I'm sorry for the pride involved in even thinking I could make this happen. Please teach me humility. Selfish pride has had such a deep root in my life; I desire to combat that with extreme humility. I'm sorry for the fear that I've given in to; please love me perfectly. I receive Your love. Go deep into my heart and love me, Lord Jesus. I trust You. As a child trusts her Father, I give You my life. Please transform me. Help me to stop obsessing about Bob, and change me. I need You.

Audrey, the Former Control Freak

If you've ever met a control freak, you know what I'm talking about. It's tiring even being within a twelve-foot radius of one, and everything in you wants to yell, "Take a chill pill!" I've always prided myself on being an easy-going and fun-loving person, and even thought about how wonderful it must be for Bob to have a wife who doesn't nag and rag on him all the time.

So you can imagine the horror I felt to discover that I was one! Not only was I a control freak; I was a perfect candidate for Control Freaks Anonymous! It only took me about twenty years of marriage to reach this point of self-discovery and, like most deep lessons in life, I wasn't ready to learn it until I was desperate for answers.

Desperation leads one to do things and pray things that otherwise would not be tackled. My day of declaration came at a time when Bob had been depressed for a particularly long season of time, and I was particularly done with it!

I love being happy and I have a personal lease on life to make sure everyone around me is happy. That way we all get to be happy and life is, well – happy! Having a husband who exuded discouragement and disdain didn't fit my equation. I thought we were doing everything we could to get this marriage healed. Bob had seasons of joy, but they were few and far between. "Something's got to give," I thought. I tried everything. I made sure the house was clean and perfect when he walked in the door. I made sure that the aroma of homemade food filtered through his nostrils. I prayed throughout the day that God's presence would fill our home, bringing joy and hope to everyone and anyone who would walk in.

My frustration came down to one haunting question, and I asked it of God: "How do I live with a depressed man?" I was crying out for the answer and was willing to do absolutely anything and everything to make it happen. I'm extremely thankful for what I learned that morning. God answered my prayer, and He answered my question. A still small voice in my heart said, "Changing Bob is not your job."

I realize that doesn't sound particularly profound, but believe me, those rhyming words have never left me. They weren't my own; they were from God Himself. There was more: The Lord did not want my passion to change Bob, He wanted me. He wanted my life, my heart, my will and my passion. I broke down and asked God to forgive me. It was as though a light turned on and I finally saw myself for the controller I really was. I was nice about it – extra sweet and generous, in fact – but my motivation was that I was out to fix everything and make everyone around me happy so that I could be happy.

Please sense the pride here. I wanted things my way because, deep down, I figured I was the best at life. Everyone needed me. When the Lord asked me to stop trying to change Bob, He told me He wanted me to look at my own heart instead. He had some changing to do right there, and repenting from pride was the first step. I must add that God shared a secret with me that still makes me smile. As I allowed Him to transform me and stopped trying to change anyone else, He promised to prepare me to become irresistible. I loved that promise!

Every man absolutely loves a woman who will stop trying to change him. It took many long years of trying before I learned this, but I'm starting to get it. It's also a paradox, because it was when I laid off trying to help Bob and fix him that things turned around in his heart! As soon as I finally stopped being obsessed with changing Bob, fixing Bob and even keeping track of Bob, I was able to release God's power into action. As I trust God relentlessly, and let Him work on my heart instead of Bob's, I become irresistible. And who doesn't want some of that?

Changing behavior takes so much effort! It's tiring! It takes retraining, extreme discipline and a lot of energy. When God changes our hearts, however, the transformation follows naturally and easily. The behavior is just the fruit on the tree. When it's a tree bearing good fruit, that good fruit is simply going to grow, multiply and bring blessing to everyone who picks and eats. I want the heart surgery! I want to plant truth in my heart so that good things grow. Effortless victory.

This is in opposition to our society at large. We are taught and stimulated to "do it ourselves." If something doesn't work right – fix it! Better yet, get the manual and just "Git-er-done." This mentality is even more dangerous when you're capable. I know my limits; when it comes to doing taxes or any kind of mechanical repair job, I'm out. I don't even want to try; I just don't have the interest.

But there's so much that I am able to do. I remember my father giving a speech at a ministry banquet, thanking me for fifteen years of service. My parents began a TV ministry when I was eleven years old which grew into a tremendously effective national entity. The speech my father gave was called, "I Can Do That." Dad recalled the time when they needed someone to write and edit the newsletter. "Audrey said, 'I can do that!' " They needed a children's TV host. "Audrey said, 'I can do that!' " They needed original songs for the show. "I can do that!" That night Dad presented me with a beautiful watch with the engraved inscription: "I can do that!"

I wore that watch proudly, knowing that my dad was proud of me, but mostly because I was proud of my own achievements. It was just a few years ago that our son David offered to clean the kitchen after dinner. The next day, when I was cleaning the kitchen, I shoved some apple peels down the garbage disposal and heard a loud clanking noise. I proceeded to pull out teeny tiny pieces of that beautiful watch!

Immediately I recognized that still small voice in my heart. God gave me instant perspective. It was time: time to stop depending on my natural abilities, talents and capabilities. God was calling me higher, to a place of dependence on Him that was supernatural. "I can do that," sure; but to be submitted to God, resting in His abilities, confident in His abiding presence, teachable to go His way and not my own brings me to a place of peace, stability and rest...rest from control.

Replacing the natural with the supernatural is what Bob and I are learning to live every day. When our marriage faced the test of adultery, our natural love ran dry. It's easy for us to understand those who walk away instead of facing the depth of pain. Yet God has an abundant supply of perfect love available for the asking. His supernatural love covers, protects, forgives, accepts, promotes, restores and redeems. That's the kind of love that saturates one into being irresistible.

Controlling Your Disappointment

We love feeling connected; it seems our relationship goes through seasons of being both connected and disconnected. Disappointment in each other is inevitable. Where you have your greatest expectations is where you'll likely experience the most disappointment. When disappointment comes, you must make a choice: Will you let it bring an offense, and thus lessen your connection with your spouse, or will you refuse to take offense and preserve that precious connection?

Too many disappointments result in a closed heart. When this happens, your desire for relationship shuts down and you have little motivation to be best friends and best lovers. A closed heart will cause you to punish the other without even knowing it by withdrawing affection, giving a cold shoulder and even becoming argumentative and accusing.

Having unrealistic expectations of each other is very normal but can also be extremely damaging. A smart thing to do is to evaluate your needs realistically, as well as your desire for your spouse to fill those needs, and then communicate. When you communicate your expectations, they have a much better chance of being realized! It's those unspoken judgments that cause a rift in your connection with each other.

Nobody likes being with someone who's disappointed in him or her! This is why so many are reluctant to approach God. They see themselves as a huge disappointment to Him and don't feel worthy to be in His Presence. We will all fail in some form or another, and we will fail each other.

Whenever you respond positively to your spouse with an attitude of acceptance and forgiveness, even when disappointed, you are participating with God's heart. It's actually His goodness that leads one to repentance. When a truly repentant heart approaches you, how can you resist? A humble heart is easily received, but even God resists the proud. It's very difficult for us to see our own shortcomings, but extremely easy to see the shortcomings of others! When Bob and I are not connected, I don't ask the Lord to change Bob, I ask Him for a new point of view! What is it in my heart that I probably can't see, but is causing my wrong attitudes and behavior?

It's the kindness of God that leads those around us to repentance, not our reminding them of their sins and weaknesses! (Romans 2:4) Often we approach repentance from a position of fear, repenting out of fear of judgment. If we fear judgment, love hasn't been perfected in us (First John 4:18-19). Our repentance allows God's goodness, grace, love and mercy to fill out hearts, and we gain a new point of view. It's a change of mind; I now see God differently, I see others differently, and I recognize my error.

The Weary and Heavy Laden: Bob's Turn

"Come to me, all you who are weary and burdened, and I will give you rest. ...For my yoke is easy and my burden is light" (Matthew 11:28-30, NIV). Those who are weary have had enough. They're tired, they're sick of this marriage and they just want to quit. They may be hiding behind façades of activity, trying to fight off the weariness and tiredness that they feel. But this is more than just an emotional problem; it is spiritually driven! The enemy would love to wear you out.

As men, we know we've been failures at being the spiritual leader and the priest of the home, so it's easy to just quit trying and become spiritually lazy. We can leave the praying and directing to our wives, they've been good at controlling the whole thing anyway. Without realizing it, men who make this decision become emotionally detached from their families. When their hearts are not in communion, they become lonely and vulnerable for someone to give them love they can feel.

After being disappointed and living with unmet expectations, it's natural to become a quitter. Excuses and blame rise up: "I'm hurt...he didn't...I wish she'd..." The enemy hands you a list of expectations for the sole purpose of dashing those expectations and bringing division into your home and marriage. The next thing to take place in this cycle of quitting is that you enter the land of the wilderness. You stop growing in your relationships, you don't feel challenged, you aren't assertive and part of you just doesn't care anymore.

We become weary and tired because what was once exciting and thrilling and new has become common. What was once holy, sacred, set apart and special has become common. No longer do we see the ways of God as holy, but we have stagnated and allowed them to become common. Common is the opposite of holy!

The others mentioned in these verses are the heavy-laden. This is the other response to disappointment. Okay, if you're going to disappoint me, or if that didn't work, we're just going to pull on our boots and make it work! Many people who have been stepped on and used and abused take on this mentality: I'm going to be independent. I refuse to let anyone control me again!

There is a different response that we can have when we've been used and abused. Take Abraham and Sarah, for example. They were a man and woman of God who traveled to a new and strange place by God's direction. They had faith. Yet Abraham lied to save his own skin, placing Sarah's life in potential jeopardy. A pagan king had his eye on Sarah. Abraham, instead of protecting her, said, "She's my sister. Take her into your harem." How crazy is that! Abraham thought the king might kill him for Sarah if he knew Sarah was his wife.

Even more astounding is Sarah's response. She prayed and said, "God, Abraham is not doing a good job of protecting me today." The Lord gave the king a dream revealing the truth, and said, "If you touch her there will be a curse on you and your nation." Sarah didn't take this against Abraham; she took it to God. She trusted him when her husband betrayed her. She was untouched. When we stop fighting against our spouse and take our requests to God, He races across heaven to do something about it!

There are many fabulous ways to control; every one of us has a tendency to control in one way or another. Some of us control through our personalities. A strong leader may dominate through power, while a naturally funny person may manipulate using humor. A depressed person can control through unhappy moods, forcing those around to join the cloud. The list could go on and on! Your personality traits are a gift from God, designed to serve those around you. Or they can be twisted and used to control.

Temper and criticism are almost always signs of a control mentality. You might find yourself saying, "Yeah, I really like that person, but there's just that one thing. He's always..." Judgment places people in boxes, forces an identity on them from our point of view and keeps them at arm's length. We also control through our opinions. Some people have an opinion about everybody – how they should clean their house, how they drive, who their friends should be, what church they should go to, how they parent their children. It is not our place to fix other people's problems! What a deception to be obsessed with others and not pay attention to our own heart! Jesus nailed it when He said: *"Why worry about a speck in your friend's eye when you have a log in your own?"* (Matthew 7:3)

Some men get married so they can control at least one person: their wife. What a motivation to enter into covenant! Wives threaten to "cut their husbands off" if they don't get that new couch they've been wanting. Parents control their children, and when the children are grown, the parents still try to control. Some control through their sexuality, knowing that there is huge power in their physical appearance – it's like a power center!

Any kind of control is cooperating with sin. It's knowing how to get what your selfish nature wants and being willing to do whatever it takes to get it. Pride and judgment say, "At least I'm not as bad, ugly, unloving, fearful, discontented, lustful or bitter as that other person!" That's the oldest trap of justification on the face of the earth, and it never has a happy ending.

Withholding affection from Audrey was my way of punishing her. I could retain control as long as I had her under my mood. Control is always based on fear, so this was my way to keep her "very sorry" for what she did, so that she wouldn't sin again! I needed her to be in fear as well, so that we could both have the guarantee that it wouldn't happen again. Outbursts of anger are always controlling, and I knew that as long as I kept her under my anger control tactic, she would be scared to be selfish again. If I kept asking, "Why did you do that?" I could keep her thinking about what she did, and how wrong it was. What I didn't realize at the time was that asking "why" is always based on a judgment. My fear-based love of punishment provoked her fear-based love of performance. This cycle would still be in full motion if it weren't for God's supernatural and perfect love that cast out all fear in giving us a new point of view.

Guilt Is Not Attractive

Controllers love to put the people around them on guilt trips. Unmet expectations just make most people angry! And when you're angry with someone, he or she can feel guilty pretty quickly! Unfortunately, guilt usually advances to the next step, where the person also feels like a worthless failure. The enemy uses guilt to wound our hearts so that we can't live a satisfied life.

Guilt is something that enslaves and puts too many people into bondage. Spending time with someone who's "guilty" is not exactly pleasurable! Unless, that is, it's someone you're attempting to control, and the guilt is all part of your plan to punish and manipulate.

If you have truly repented before God, and have asked Jesus to forgive you and cleanse you, it is in your best interest to believe that He has! Living in the guilt of the mistakes you have made is actually agreeing with the enemy.

There's Hope!

Jesus wants to change your heart. When He does, your attitude will change too. Instead of participating with pride that controls, you can embrace a humble attitude and relinquish your rights. In doing so you will find rest for your soul! There is nothing more satisfying than being at perfect rest: rest from comparing yourself to others, from judging others and from criticizing. I'm convinced that such rest from control will slow down the aging process and allow you to live longer! It will definitely make you irresistible to those around you, especially to your spouse.

There is ministry going on for you continually at the throne of God. Jesus is interceding for you. Satan wants to accuse you, but he doesn't have access to God's throne, so he uses other people, often other Christians, to accuse you in judgment. As you continue to accuse yourself and others, you just help him along, aiding the enemy in his business. On the other hand, as you receive God's beautiful peace, forgiveness and acceptance and begin to learn to see yourself as He sees you, you connect with the heart of Jesus. As you pray for others, including your spouse and children, and intercede on their behalf even when they've disappointed you, you are in right relationship. This is a great way to be a best friend and to participate with God's ministry!

Are you committed to being connected to your spouse? If you've had a change of thought, then you can have a change of action. Otherwise, you're just trying to change your actions while continuing to think wrongly about yourself, God and others! Offenses and disappointments are perfect opportunities to inject the glory of God into your relationships. These are the perfect places to mature, to die to yourself and to get more of God. That's the great exchange, the mysterious secret that leads to complete fulfillment and unending satisfaction.

God loves changing our hearts. When we are inspired to change, we prepare ourselves for behavioral changes. We create lists, charts, goals and projections. These things are fine and good in some areas. However, when it comes to massive transformation – a total change –

then it must take place in our hearts. God promises to give us a new heart with new desires. That's a good thing, because when we know what we want, we usually go after it with strength and determination. Since we can be fairly strong-willed and determined, we want to be sure our desires are good and safe ones. Since we're likely to get what we go after, let's go after the heart of God! Be free from control and free from controlling your spouse. Your best days of rest are ahead!

So when things become challenging, expectations are not met and you're living through hurt and pain in your relationship, you can rest in God and adopt His attitude for your own. You can relinquish your rights. When you do these things in the Lord there's an inner resilience. His load really is light when you are fully dependent on Him.

Get together with Jesus as your very best Friend. The best way to be best friends with your spouse is to be best friends with Him first. As you listen to His voice, He'll tell you powerful secrets of His wisdom concerning how to have great relationships. Pour out your feelings to Him. Maybe you're full of joy! Maybe you're really sad; maybe you're not in the mood to talk. Whatever you're experiencing, just be honest with Him! He'll meet you at that place and be with you. When you have Jesus as your best Friend, it is nothing short of having heaven on earth!

Heart Revelation: The Tough Questions

In what ways have I been controlling, and how will I pursue a heart transformation?

What disappointment am I struggling with right now, and what right choices do I need to make to restore a right relationship?

Do I recognize prayer with my spouse as a needed discipline for my marriage?

Heart transformation: The Truth Established

Abstaining from controlling and fixing my spouse is my first priority and step in becoming irresistible. (See Mark 11:24-25.)

146

God's perfect love has no fear. If there is no fear, I will not need to control! (See Hebrews 13:6.)

Trusting God is a gift to Him: It is telling Him that I really do believe who He says He is, and that what He says, He'll do. (See Romans 10:17.)

My personality is a gift to those around me. The Lord can teach me to use it for His glory! (See First Peter 4:10.)

I will find true rest for my soul as I relinquish my rights. (See Isaiah 26:3.)

As I intercede and pray blessing over my spouse, I am agreeing with God and His intercession! (See Ephesians 3:12.)

Prayer

Dear Father in Heaven, I receive Your amazing grace to my racing mind and every tired cell of my body. I need Your rest in my emotional and spiritual life. Thank You that I can find rest in You, deep rest in my heart. Please lift the hurt, disappointment and unrealistic expectations that I have held close. I choose to depend on You completely and find Your rest and peace. You give me a peace not like the world gives; I have no need to be troubled or afraid.

I confess to You that when things haven't gone my way, I've been angry, hurt and moody. I come to You in humility right now and reach out for Your grace. I break the power of control that has hooked itself to my hurts, trauma and disappointment. Instead of being angry, I trust You. Please take care of me and lead me, as I trust You.

I will not doubt or fear others' judgments. I ask for healing, wholeness and restoration according to Your will. Even if restoration doesn't look like I thought it would, I know it's still there! I know that You have my best interest in mind because You love me.

Screaming Freedom: It's All Because We Pray

Audrey and I were ministering to a group who all attended the same church. I gave the men permission to ask each other on any given Sunday, "Are you doing it?" What I was referring to was praying together. This is something we're adamant about! Whether your marriage is absolutely great or on the verge of separation, there really isn't an option as to how important this daily communion is. Being a guy, I can press into the guys about leading this time of prayer. I see all the women's eyes light up; I can almost hear their thoughts: "Thank you! I've wanted him to pray with me for years!" I then describe this time as being short and simple.

"As you gaze into each other's eyes, find the life of Jesus in your mate. Pray to God, but look at your spouse. Men start and thank God for anything that's on your heart. Women, do the same. Then, men, humble yourselves and repent. Ask forgiveness for any offense. Women, do the same. Finally, men, pray a blessing, and the women follow." Women constantly tell us that they feel closer and more in love with their husbands when they take this step with them on a daily basis.

One pastor contacted us four months after we gave this exercise to his church. He proclaimed that the entire spiritual climate of the church family had ignited as a result of this simple time of daily prayer between couples. God is faithful and longs to answer the prayers of His people!

7

SETTLED TRUST

It is natural to trust the people you know. Getting to know God more deeply will deepen your trust in Him and activate faith and hope in your life in a very natural way. This will strengthen your prayer: "I want to be best friends and lovers with my spouse!"

The best way to get to know each other is to spend time together hearing God's voice moment by moment. We all have two sets of eyes: our physical or natural eyes, and the eyes of our heart, with which we see into the spiritual realm. Paul says, *"I pray…that the eyes of your heart may be enlightened…"* (Ephesians 1:18, NIV) Our eyes are the windows to our heart.

One of the greatest prerequisites for hearing God's voice and following Him in a supernatural lifestyle is desire. Our very desire for Him and to know Him creates an appetite for more. We've all heard stories on the sports networks of how the winners are always the teams or individuals who were the hungriest for victory. In the same way, we must have an appetite for more of God, to see Him in our hearts and in the world around us. If we struggle with even having an appetite, then we need to be asking ourselves, "What does my diet consist of? Is my life too much of a mixture? Do I want the ways of God but continue to live my life with the ways of the world and begin to adopt its point of view?" For many it's too much television. We want you to begin to dream again and have vision for your marriage. But if you don't begin to gain

God's point of view, then "tel-e-vision" will certainly give you one! Jesus said, *"Blessed are those who hunger and thirst for righteousness, for they will be filled"* (Matthew 5:6, NIV). Righteousness is the very nature and character of God. How hungry are you?

His Treasure

Years ago, when I, Audrey, first started journaling, I asked God how He felt about me. That was definitely the beginning of the rest of my life! Everything changed when I discovered my value in Him. He spoke words of identity, worth and beauty to me. I was His treasure! Knowing how precious I am to Him helps me feel completely secure in relationships and totally satisfied in Him.

The same is true for your marriage! You cannot give value to your spouse if you have no value to give. Being married to someone who values you is a bit of heaven on earth. Unfortunately, almost every human being struggles with his or her own value when it comes to the deep issues of the heart. Our inherent need as humans is to feel significant in this world. The enemy works hard to tempt us with false idols that promise value but deliver nothing.

What are these idols? A few that come to mind are a successful profession or business, a fit and healthy body, wealth and riches, fame, beauty, education, children and family and effective ministry. Of course, there are many others. Some of you may be thinking, "Well, what's wrong with those? They all sound pretty good to me!" You're right; there is nothing wrong with any of these things – as long as you do not draw your sense of personal value and worth from them! If you do, that is an indication of a heart problem. Your personal identity – how you see yourself – derives from what you value the most.

Your identity also lies at the core of how you live your life. As wonderful as these things may be to have in and of themselves, you will never discover your true identity or value by pursuing them. Knowledge of your identity and value lies elsewhere. This is actually good news. What if you never acquire some of these things? You could end up wasting your life trying to find personal value in something that can never give it to you. My identity is connected solely to the love of my heavenly Father. Because He values me, loves me, adores me, protects me and promotes me, I am immune from the world's opinions. I am free from disaster, for I will always be His.

What about failure? What happens when your children mess up? When you face financial bankruptcy? Destroyed reputation? What about unfulfilled plans and dreams? If you are trusting in idols, any of these failures or setbacks can send you into a tailspin, leaving you feeling worthless and possibly even suicidal! Yet you cling desperately to your idols because they provide the only sense of worth you have, and without them you are truly lost.

There is a better way! Deriving your identity from the knowledge that you are a daughter or son of the King will keep your heart satisfied in His worth; not only in how worthy He is, but also the worth He places on you! You belong to Him and nothing will ever separate you from His love (Romans 8:38-39). Enjoy your success; work hard toward fitness, beauty and education; revel in the love of your children and spouse; press on toward effective ministry; but remember Who defines you. It is God in heaven, and He adores you!

Do I Make You Feel Worthless?

The best way to devalue your spouse is to take over. The great takeover says, "You're not good enough, smart enough or fast enough. Just let me do it." Give your spouse room to be amazing. He or she may just surprise you! Celebrate his strengths. Understand her passions. Encourage him in the daily walk of life. Celebrate her triumphs. You have the opportunity to love, value and appreciate your spouse like none other. Take advantage of this divine calling! Be a best friend and a best lover – and enjoy the rewards!

You Are Valuable

If you struggle with feeling valuable, there's a good possibility it isn't a new problem. The experts tell us that most of life's lessons are learned by age five. We have a little guy around now, as well as three much older children, and we can see what a sponge he is! His name is Robert, so we have our own personal Sponge-Bob. He absorbs everything around him: every word, every lesson, every correction, everything that makes people laugh, every observation. He doesn't miss a thing!

When he was just learning to talk, we taught him that "Meisners share." You see, there are a lot of things that Meisners just do, and if you are one, there's no question. Meisners forgive, tell the truth, obey their parents, don't talk back and eat their vegetables, to mention a few things. These truths have been established deeply into Robert's heart, and we have seen that when his heart understands, appropriate behavior comes naturally.

We recognize the importance of establishing the truth of God's character in Robert's heart at a young age, so that his heart will be molded in truth: God will never leave you. He always keeps His promises. He forgives you completely when you ask Him. He's always good. He loves you more than anyone else ever could, and there's nothing you could do that would change His love for you. You have nothing to fear with Jesus as your best friend. He wants to walk and talk with you every single day and moment of your life, and you can hear His voice and know His presence – even though He's invisible!

On the negative side, I sometimes hear myself saying things to Robert such as, "I can't play right now, I have to work." As his mom, I try to explain how happy I am to be home with him all day, and thankful that someone else isn't looking after him. Then I try to reinforce how important he is, even though I can't spend every moment with him. I know that if I am not careful, my working could impress on his heart feelings such as, "Mommy loves her work more than me. She values her job more than me. She helps everyone else around, but doesn't help me.

She's always on the phone because I'm not good enough for her."

There is great power in first introductions, or the way we are introduced to something or someone for the first time. First impressions are lasting impressions. So many people today try to avoid God, or are afraid of God, or angry at God, or hate God because their first introduction to God, their first impression, was negative: "God's mad at you. You're going to hell. You better be careful, or God will get you." First introductions are so powerful because they become established in our hearts as perceived truth. Perceived truth, even if it's wrong (and sometimes especially because it is wrong), is not easily revoked, and will affect every decision we make and every thought we think for the rest of our lives.

First introductions affect the way we think about everything: friendship, love, money, sex, you name it. Thinking back on the first introductions in your life may help you understand your heart today. Are you fearful of lack of finances? What was your heart taught at a young age? Do you see yourself as worthless and without value? What situation could have written this on your heart? Are you scared of intimacy? Were you rejected? Were you abused? How were you first introduced to sex?

We say this, not for the purpose of placing blame, but rather to foster understanding. We live out of our hearts, and what's written there could be forcing us to travel a vicious circle in which we try to change, but fail because we won't allow God to transform our hearts.

Why Can't We Be Friends?: Audrey

Having friends and being a friend both impart to us a huge sense of value and acceptance, not to mention identity! As a woman, I know how easy it is to become absorbed into friendships with other women. This is a good thing! I find that other girls who love to talk stimulate great things in me, and I have opportunity to invest encouragement and love into them. I'm talking about healthy, stimulating, purposeful relationships that are necessary for me to live a balanced life.

There was a time earlier in our marriage when my priorities weren't properly established, and my best friend and I became a little too absorbed. We talked several times a day for long periods. Our children were toddlers, our husbands were busy at work, and we found strength, laughter and joy in our friendship together.

It all seemed to be a winning situation, especially since I put less pressure on Bob to be my social life. In fact, by the time he got home from work, I had already discussed the challenges of the day, communicated all the cute things our kids had said, and thrashed out the solutions to problems. My girlfriend and I talked about everything: our husbands, our intimacy issues, our heart's cries. We were bonded.

What I didn't realize was that I was filling my need for Bob with someone else. I really wanted Bob to be my best friend, but this was much more convenient. My girlfriend seemed to understand me better and things were natural and easy between us. I was robbing Bob of the intimate details of my life and was completely unaware of any problem.

Because this girl and I had a shared faith and love for God, I couldn't imagine how it could be unhealthy. One day God asked me to look at the relationship from His point of view. He asked me to reason with Him and consider how this could be dangerous. I did...and it was. The light turned on and I unexpectedly had a new point of view.

I suddenly saw how lonely Bob was and how he yearned for companionship beyond what I was giving him. I felt so satisfied in my relationship with this girlfriend that I had no yearning or desire for Bob to be my closest confidante. The circumstances didn't change, but my heart did – instantly.

I asked Bob to forgive me for my insensitivity. I told him that I wanted him more than any other friend in this world. I would give him my heart, my strengths, my weaknesses, my laughter, my vulnerability, my secrets. He smiled and lovingly received me. I didn't have to drop the friendship with the girlfriend; the change had already happened in my heart. It was back where it should have been all along.

Guys definitely need their macho time, I'm sure, although Bob's never been one to hang out with other guys. Just as with girlfriends, this is healthy and fine as long as "guy time" doesn't steal away precious moments that men should reserve for their wives or waste valuable time they should be spending with their children.

Guys, the way to initiate a change in this regard is not through behavior modification, but heart transformation. The Lord will give you a new heart filled with new desires to spend time with your wife. The truth is that there is no one more anointed on this earth to fulfill you and give you enjoyment than the wife of your youth!

Friendship with Your Father

The friendship of the heavenly Father offers you the ultimate source of value and identity. Scripture reveals how the Lord compares His love for His people to a father's love for his son. He remembers how He cared for Israel in his youth and mourns that His son has turned away from Him. Hosea 11:8 is one of the deepest cries of love from the heart of God that we find in the Bible. His heart is breaking over his wayward son:

> Oh, how can I give you up, Israel? How can I let you go? How can I destroy you like Admah and Zeboiim? My heart is torn within me, and my compassion overflows.
> Hosea 11:8

Families provide the context for the greatest sources of both joy and pain. Those who have experienced rejection by a son or daughter or abandonment by a parent know the meaning of pain! And the enemy has been having a heyday infusing God's children with a deep sense of worthlessness, paralyzing them from receiving their heavenly Father's perfect love.

In the family of God there is no place of lack, no lost identity. We are missing out on our inheritance because of a wrong identity; there has been an epidemic of spiritual identity theft! The enemy has fed us lies and they have taken root in our hearts, resulting in deeply entrenched feelings of guilt, fear and self-hatred. It's time for us to be liberated!

The Abundant Life, Ripe for the Picking!: Bob

So the fight is on! Will we walk into the abundant life that remains for us to experience? Whether we like it or not, spiritual warfare plays

Let this message burrow deep into your spirit: God wants to write His truth on your heart.

a big part in our receiving and keeping our healing. The devil does not want to see us made whole. Jesus Himself said that Satan has been a liar from the beginning. And many of his lies are aimed squarely at robbing us of the salvation and wholeness of life God has given us. Let this message burrow deep into your spirit: God wants to write His truth on your heart.

The apostle Paul, writing to the church at Corinth to address these kinds of problems, said:

> *We are human, but we don't wage war with human plans and methods. We use God's mighty weapons, not mere worldly weapons, to knock down the Devil's strongholds. With these weapons we break down every proud argument that keeps people from knowing God. With these weapons we conquer their rebellious ideas, and we teach them to obey Christ.*
> Second Corinthians 10:3-5

Throughout his letters Paul saw the problems of the people not merely as personal disorders, emotional difficulties or leadership conflicts, but as demonic attempts by Satan to attack God's people.

There's not a Christian alive who has failed to experience one of these attacks. Satan does all he can to hurt us by hurling lies against our minds. When we fail to use our spiritual resources to dislodge and do away with these thoughts, they take root in our minds and become entrenched there. The Bible calls them *strongholds*. A stronghold is any lie that keeps us from embracing the love and acceptance of Jesus and works against us in every life-giving relationship. This includes our marriages!

Satan's power is in the lies he tells us. He doesn't work with truth; he works with deception. Jesus said Satan cannot hold to the truth, *"for there is no truth in him"* (John 8:44). He lies to us about others, leading us to prejudge them; he lies to us about who we are or how we must perform. He calls into question the character of God and who He is. All of these lies can keep us from the knowledge of Christ.

Since Satan's weapons against us are based on lies, our only defense against him is truth. Our combat with the enemy isn't some cosmic arm-wrestling match; it is a truth encounter. When we speak truth from our inherited place of authority in Christ we expose Satan's lies and gain power over him. We are not saved by information about the truth, but by revelation born out of desperation, which leads to transformation.

In seasons of deep crisis our lives seem to be bombarded with intense emotions. Attached to these emotions are thoughts often associated with non-truth. We don't necessarily see them that way, for they are hidden in emotion. If these emotions go unchecked, the lies attached to them can become a foothold for the schemes of the enemy for our lives. Although we may not believe them consciously, they are being written on our hearts, where we accept them as truth, and they then develop into a belief system.

Emotional lies might include deep insecurity, shame, guilt or fear. Each one of these that is unresolved, buried and simply not dealt with will eventually take root in our lives. Then the enemy will take the platform to reinforce these lies about others, ourselves and God. The result is a stronghold. To detect a stronghold in your life you must first know the truth.

This is where my journey to freedom began. There was a crisis (my wife's infidelity) that brought me to a point of near despair. I soon discovered that my strength and abilities were not adequate for the days that would follow. Every previous lie that had been written on my heart arose to be validated. "Who has ever really been committed to you unconditionally? There is no one." "Who can you trust, honestly? There is no one." The lie within the emotion of disappointment is to undermine your confidence in a promise. And it is able to take on a tremendous force and power of its own to stand between you and others, including your spouse, your children and God.

There is a basic lie at the root of all patterns of selfishness. That lie is that we will find our significance or forgiveness or overcome guilt or fear or shame or find importance in something we do or don't do. The truth, however, is that we will find our healing in the love of our Heavenly Father. I want to help you connect with the love of your Father. God planted the Tree of Life in the garden of Eden. But all too often our life is a tree of death that grows from the soil where we have sown seeds of unresolved emotional pain.

There are four emotions that I have found are common to most people that result either from their own wrong choices, leading to sin, or from the sinful behavior of others against them.

Anger

Another word that is often used to describe anger is *temper*. The original meaning of the word is very interesting; we use it to describe the process of hardening steel. Anger is meant to harden us to face the crisis the way steel is hardened when it is tempered. But if our emotions go unchecked, and the energy that is generated by our anger is allowed to go wild, we then say, "I lost my temper," which is actually what happened. We have lost our ability to handle ourselves.

Anger as a behavior is often a person's response to rejection or abandonment and usually includes a desire to get even. Anger as a feeling, however, is in itself morally neutral. It can lead either to sinful behavior or to righteous behavior.

So how do you know if your anger is justified in the first place? Good question. What is your perspective? What is your point of view? Do you feel threatened? Do you sense danger? What is it that you want to protect? What is of utmost importance that is demanding your defense?

All too often the answer to these questions is: me. My pride. My ego. My opinion.

We must rightly discern between feelings and behavior to see how anger can move us toward reconciliation. If there has been an offense or wrongdoing that needs to be dealt with, we need to do so with honesty and compassion. We must deal with the issue square on with no attempts to skirt around it before the matter of forgiveness can be dealt with.

In fact, premature forgiveness or an attempt to lessen the unpleasantness of the moment will result in the whole thing being buried. The same thing happens when you've been unjustly treated and you're afraid of anger, so you repress it before it has a chance to express itself. In both cases anger moves underground. There it smolders, generating resentment that will be felt over and over again. Left unattended, resentment will produce malice, bitterness and depression.

Here is some surprising news. You will not shock God if you tell Him exactly how you feel about someone. I have discovered that He wants me to express my deep emotion; it's that important! The Bible says, " 'Come now, let us reason together,' says the Lord" (Isaiah 1:18, NIV). The Lord wants us to express our emotions so that we can gain a new point of view! Becoming so entangled in conflicting emotion that we don't know where to turn or what to do can be truly treacherous. And nothing is more frightening than trying to hold on even as you feel the firm foundation of truth being pulled out from under you! It is in places such as these that we need to discover a new point of view.

Fear

Fear enters our hearts in many different ways. It can come through rejection, abandonment, abuse, legalism, or even non-communication. Fear can result from unintended offenses. These are the little things that those who are close to us may do that hit us the wrong way. Fear can lodge itself in our heart through a traumatic event of life. It can come also through sexual or verbal abuse. Exposure to authoritarian leadership can cause us to lose our confidence and feel fearful.

Some fears are good because they warn us of danger. For example, the fear of the unknown, of heights, of death or of fire can all be used in positive ways, warning us to avoid things that may be dangerous. However, these very same fears can be driven to an extreme and become quite paralyzing, robbing us of our ability to function with joy.

Fear can cripple when it causes us to start believing a lie. Fear will drive us to do anything we can to avoid rejection and find approval. Pain and fear go hand in hand, and the fear of rejection is one of the greatest fears of all.

Fear lives in our hearts because our hearts have not been perfected in love:

God is love…There is no fear in love. But perfect love drives out fear, because fear has to do with punishment. The one who fears is not made perfect in love.
First John 4:16-18, NIV

I believe the Word of God. There is no fear in love. Perfect love drives out fear. Thank You, Father God, that there is hope for me in overcoming my fears!

Guilt

When guilt goes unresolved it can produce in us tremendous fear, alienation and confusion. Some people respond to guilt like a dog that has been repeatedly beaten by its owner for misbehavior. They feel put down and worthless. The emotion of guilt, whether false or true, leads to the lie, "I must avoid failure; failure is my fault." Guilt-driven people are performers. They feel that they must atone for their failures; they must overcome their weakness and show that they are all right. Because of their weak or wrong concepts of God they work hard to obtain a sense of approval. And because of their deep-seated sense of worthlessness, each failure is compounded by their failures of the past.

God has an answer for your guilt. Please receive it. I know you don't deserve it; who does? But it is a given remedy for your destructive cycle of performance and being guilt-ridden, believing the lie that your behavior defines you. Christ took the guilt of our sin, placed it upon Himself and carried it to the cross. He died and took the punishment we deserved. Why? Immense, infinite love and never-ending mercy. He designed us for right relations with Himself and with each other.

So now there is no condemnation for those who belong to Christ Jesus. For the power of the life-giving Spirit has freed you through Christ Jesus from the power of sin that leads to death.
Romans 8:1-3

Shame

Shame is a sense of hopelessness, a feeling that we cannot change; that there is no alternative for us. It is connected to our identity and is related directly to our self-esteem, or the way we see ourselves. Shame says, "That's the way you are. You cannot change. You will always be like this." Shame leads to feelings of passivity, self-pity, destructive behavior, feelings of inferiority, withdrawal, anger toward others, loss of creativity and unhealthy dependence on people. Those people who experience shame struggle with hopelessness. They feel worthless, convinced that they are failures.

Self-condemnation robs us of godly conviction and leaves us with a feeling of shame and worthlessness. God-inspired conviction is intended to lead us to a profound repentance that takes us to a place where we can begin to exchange the lie for the truth. Paul wrote:

For the sorrow that is according to the will of God produces a repentance without regret, leading to salvation, but the sorrow of the world produces death.
Second Corinthians 7:10, NASB

Shame is a garment that others want to place on you to ensure you know what wrong or offense you have committed. The power of this false identity will be broken as you make your way to Jesus and ask Him for new sight. Then you can see how others are trying to manipulate you and place their identity upon you. I pray you will receive a new point of view and revelation of God's great love and acceptance of you as His dearly beloved.

For his Holy Spirit speaks to us deep in our hearts and tells us that we are God's children. And since we are his children, we will share his treasures – for everything God gives to his Son, Christ, is ours, too.
Romans 8:16-17a

Turn up the Truth

Learn to focus on the love of God in your life. Practice meditating on positive truths: God can use me. I am an heir of the King. People are attracted to the very life of God that dwells within me. I love my wife or husband. I'm a new creature in Christ Jesus. I am bound neither by my past nor by the past of previous generations. The cross of Christ was more than enough. It is finished. I am His child and I can hear and know His voice when He speaks to me.

As you take time to focus on God's love, learn also to be wise to the schemes of the enemy who would love to take the good and necessary and turn it around and cause it to be destructive. We can become so focused on what God can do for us that we actually become "selfish in love." Yet a proper and true understanding of God's love will always lead us to focus on serving others. By its very nature, love is unselfish.

God heals us so that we can go into the entire world to be instruments of healing for others. He has called us to be reconcilers.

Reconcile People, Not Problems: Bob

The standard clinical approach to reconciliation is really quite simple: Identify the problem, develop possible solutions, select the best solution, apply that solution and presto! We are now reconciled!

Great plan – except that it doesn't work. A relationship that has been going downhill for a long time has become so enmeshed in he said/she said claims and counterclaims that it becomes all but impossible to discern objective truth. At this stage of deterioration, the relational problems are too deep and too complex to be solved quickly and painlessly through the use of a pat formula. Besides, the very strain of the problem-solving process itself can push an already stressed relationship to the breaking point. Even if the problem-solving process succeeds in establishing some facts and clearing some of the muddy water, it will usually be at the expense of one partner over the other. One partner will come away feeling justified while the other is left feeling humiliated, stripped naked and ashamed. This may well prove more than the beleaguered couple can bear.

If identifying and solving the problem is not the right approach to reconciliation, then what is? To find the answer, we need to look again at God's approach to reconciliation. When God seeks to reconcile, He doesn't focus first on problem solving. Besides, through the death of Christ His Son, God has already solved our biggest problem: our alienation from Him because of our sin. He doesn't require us to deal first with our life problems before we become reconciled with Him. In fact, when we first turn to God we don't know what our real problems are anyway. We may recognize the presence of a sense of alienation between ourselves and God and other people, but awareness of our true problems comes only much later, after the Holy Spirit has brought us to the place of being able to look at our own hearts honestly and objectively.

How then does God reconcile us? He does it by pursuing us. When we are alienated and separated from God, He comes to us. He finds us in the midst of our confusion and despair and lostness and leads us home again. When God confronted Adam about his rebellion in the garden of Eden He didn't start off by asking, "What have you done?" He asked Adam, "Where are you?" That is a relational question, not a problem-solving question. In the same way, Jesus left heaven and came to earth looking for us. He came not to solve problems, but to restore a broken relationship.

> We must deal with our thoughts, imaginations and dreams that are based on sin from the very beginning in order to be protected from the schemes of the enemy.

Problem solving is one of the results of reconciliation; it is not the means of reconciliation. Often after Audrey and I share our testimony and teach about marriage, people come up to me and say, "Wow, Bob! I could never do that!" My response is always the same: "Yeah, you're right, and neither could I. It's impossible!" Then I say, "But God can, and He did!" I could never have reconciled with Audrey on my own. I'm not that good, I'm not that smart and I'm definitely not that loving. But God is merciful and did in us what we could never have done for ourselves. Even today when I look back over it all I sit back in amazement and say, "Wow! God did that!" It completely blows me away.

I know how totally and completely reconciled I am to the Lord, and He to me. When I see the cross and everything Christ did for me, and when I think about having experienced His unconditional love, and knowing that He has given me this great gift and opportunity of reconciling the world to Him – in the face of all this, how can I not be reconciled to my wife and family?

When I look at the cross, I don't see an answer; I see God coming after me in relentless, unconditional love, making a way. Once I see the transforming power of the cross at work in my life, I can translate that same power into my relationships.

Reconcile God's Way

Best friends and best lovers reconcile their differences. If you want to become irresistible to each other again and be satisfied in a right relationship full of richness, fruitfulness and joy, resolve to reconcile God's way. First, take time to find each other again. Lay aside all of your disagreements and differences. There will be time to deal with those later, when both of you have closed the distance between yourselves and can approach them from a common and less emotionally-charged perspective. As long as you remain focused on your maze of accumulated problems you will never find common ground.

Agree together to set your differences aside and entrust yourselves to the grace of God.

Once you come together face to face in the presence of a loving God, He will begin to help you to understand the factors that have caused your separation from each other. You may come to realize that you have stopped relating to each other as people and started judging each other by behavior alone. All the things you have always liked about each other have been eclipsed by pain and anger over injuries perceived or real, misunderstandings, disagreements and the destructive impulse to retaliate. Choosing beforehand to walk the road to reconciliation together makes it easier to face the harsh realities of the process because you know you are not alone. Even in estrangement there is a level of comfort in companionship.

The second important point in being reconciled God's way is to recognize the vital role of grace. Because God has been gracious to you in Christ, you can afford to extend grace to each other. From the perspective of grace there is always hope – not just for survival, but also for full reconciliation. Right after I learned of Audrey's adultery, I could not see a happy solution for our situation. I was willing to settle as best we could and simply survive. We were nothing more than damaged goods, dependent on God's mercy but devoid of His grace. Sin wanted to have its way with us by holding us in a mindset of irreconcilable differences. There we would be ineffective and unproductive in our lives.

That is why we had to run to the Father and ask for grace. In humility we draw near to Him, press in and lean heavily on His ability as we become dependent on Him. To know God's grace you must know His love. You must realize His total acceptance of you or else you will never be able to receive His grace. The starting place for receiving the strength of the Lord is realizing your own weakness and admitting that you cannot do the will of God in your own power. In a supernatural battle your natural power is useless. Don't depend on your own strength. Instead, seek to *"be strong in the Lord's mighty power"* (Ephesians 6:10).

Open yourselves up to the wonderful prospect of rediscovering a deep sense of value in one another. Because each of you is worth saving as a person, your marriage is worth saving also. You will also rediscover a curiosity to know each other and to be known.

Admit and recognize to one another your need for mutual change. You can now commit yourselves to face the necessary changes that reconciliation undoubtedly will bring and help each other through those changes no matter how uncomfortable and difficult they may seem initially.

Once you enter the reconciliation process together you will begin to experience divine grace at work that will lead you to a new beginning. A whole new dynamic is at work. The relationship that emerges will be new, fresh, dynamic and much stronger than before because it will be founded on the divine principles of grace, mercy, love and covenant commitment.

You are exceptional, purposeful and irresistible. You may not believe these things about yourself, but the treasure of your true identity and your intrinsic value is hidden in the depths of your heart. It waits to be discovered when your heart is satisfied in God, for it is then that you will be able to cease from struggling and striving and know your place of rest and peace. Your Father in heaven loves you deeply; believing that may be a tremendous obstacle for you, but it is still true.

When our little guy was born, I gave him my name. Will there be times in his life when he will have to fight to be assured of my love for him? Probably, simply because of the nature of the circumstances in which he was conceived (in adultery). However, we can write words of truth on his heart now that will establish his place in God's kingdom, as a son in whom I am well pleased, loved by His father in heaven and extravagantly valued for his place in the kingdom. I refuse to participate in a fatherless generation by ever questioning my role as Robert's father. I will passionately love him for his entire life and will pursue him, just as my Father in heaven pursues me.

We recently went out for a very expensive dinner for our anniversary. I felt slightly uncomfortable walking into the restaurant, knowing that this was "high end" stuff we were dealing with! After we had eaten a couple of pieces of bread and tried to figure out the menu, one of the servers quickly took a special brush and dealt with the crumbs that had fallen onto the tablecloth. Three hours of uninterrupted conversation allowed for plenty of time to cover many topics of discussion! Something we put into words for the first time was this: We both fight. Every day, we fight to maintain God's point of view. We fight to know our worth in God our Father. We fight to stay in agreement with His identity for us. We refuse to let daily circumstances and encounters steal the value that our Father in Heaven has placed on us. We encourage you to do the same: Refuse to believe the lie, and fight for truth in your life. Your marriage as best friends and best lovers depends on it!

Heart Revelation: The Tough Questions

Are there some things about your body or personality that have made you feel different from other people, as though you don't fit in?

Have there been situations in your life where feeling different has led you to feel inferior to others?

Read Psalm 139:13-14 aloud to yourself. Can you agree with what this Scripture says about the way God made you?

What are some gifts God has given you that you can use in either a constructive or a destructive way?

You trust who you know. Are you committed to knowing God in an ever-increasing level of intimacy?

Do you allow your achievements, looks or position to determine your value and identity?

Heart Transformation: The Truth Established

God is your heavenly Father. He loves you, accepts you and values you more than words could describe. He created us to need and know His love! (See First John 1:3.)

When we are emptied of His love, we don't know his character. To combat this we can spend our days getting to know Him more deeply every day! (See Matthew 11:28-30.)

You are a son or daughter of the King. That makes you royalty, a privileged one, with continual access to your Father. (See Luke 15:17-18.)

Every problem or challenge we face can be overcome by a greater understanding of God's character. (See Revelation 2:4-5.)

Once I see the transforming power of the cross at work in my life, I can translate that same power into my relationships. (See First John 1:9.)

From the perspective of grace there is always hope not just for survival, but also for full reconciliation. (Hebrews 7:25.)

Prayer

Father, I need You so badly. I don't know how I'm going to make it through this day. The demands on me are more than I can bear.

Without You, I have nothing, and I am nothing. However, I choose to ignite faith in my heart and receive Your love. With You, I have everything, and I am Your very precious child. Father, please provide for me today. I refuse to live out of a sense of lack! I receive the resources I need for the day. Your peace, Your guidance, Your wisdom, Your joy, Your patience, Your provision, Your favor, and most of all, Your love. These are Your characteristics. Not only are You my Father, but You live Your life through me.

I confess my fears to You. My health issues, my fear of not completing the tasks ahead of me, my fear of self-sufficiency, my fear of lack of finances, my fear of being rejected. Cleanse my heart completely, and give me a new heart with new desires. Give me a heart that easily receives Your provision and love in every way, and then lives accordingly. Thank You for Your perfect peace, Your outrageous joy and Your never-ending mercy. Thank You that my needs are met, and my marriage is in Your hands.

Settled Trust: In a Fatherless Generation

A couple from Germany emailed us. He was posted there with the U.S. military and he and his wife had gone through circumstances similar to ours. His wife committed adultery and became pregnant. They already had a four-year-old child, and the Lord gave them grace to stay together and keep this new baby. His wife went into the hospital and gave birth to a baby boy. After being in the hospital all night, this man went home to take a shower and grab a cup of coffee. During those few minutes, he turned on the television and saw us giving our testimony. He went back to the hospital that day full of newfound hope and healing, and began to quote what Bob had said: "This is my son. I am going to be thankful for him, and he is a gift to our family. We will not participate in a fatherless generation!" Our Father in heaven races across heaven to touch us, to teach us, to reassure us that we are not alone, and He values us deeply.

8

SOARING TOGETHER

You've made it to Chapter Eight! Eight represents new beginnings, and our dream and prayer for you to have a fresh start is a reality. When you started, maybe your marriage was trudging along, but we know that as you are applying truth and heart transformation, you are gaining speed and are about to take off. We knew you could make it! Prepare for your departure...because no eye has seen, no ear has heard, and no mind can know what God has in store for those who love Him! (See First Corinthians 2:9.) Begin to notice the changes that are taking place! You are taking a leap of faith. God will honor your courage and your confidence in Him to take you from a place of wandering to a place called the Promised Land, where you will enjoy a marriage of being best friends and best lovers!

Everyone in the Meisner family loves a good roller coaster except me – Audrey. As our kids would be the first to tell you, we have stories. I don't do well with twisting, turning and dropping; let's just leave it at that! However, there is one four-minute ride at California Adventure that I wish lasted for four hours: "Soaring over California." This ride lifts you into the Imax screen where you soar over the state, feeling the breeze, smelling the aroma of the great outdoors...you really feel like you're flying! I take my shoes off so I can feel the wind between my toes, and I soak up every second of enjoyment in hopes of making it last. It's the only ride that Bob doesn't do so well on. While I'm leaning into the screen, he's hanging on to his seatbelt for dear life. Many people I talk to fly in their dreams, and humans have been intrigued by the idea of it for all of history! Getting off the ground means going the distance, covering territory, facing fear and beginning to soar.

> ✿
>
> *Getting off the ground means going the distance, covering territory, facing fear and beginning to soar.*

It takes a lot of determination to rise to the heights and reach for the stars. Flying like an eagle, running and not growing weary, walking and not fainting at all. In order to be best friends and best lovers in your marriage, you must have intimacy. From a place of security, you can invite your spouse into a place of "in-to-me-see" (intimacy). You have a better understanding of covenant and this life-long relationship you will spend with each other.

This isn't a sprint; it's a marathon! It takes a lifetime to flourish in love. It takes a lifetime to discover the treasure of knowing and understanding one another. It takes a lifetime of opportunity to respect and honor one another. You have been given a lifetime to mature in your trust for one another. And it takes a huge amount of courage to be vulnerable and self-disclosing. These are the foundations of a healthy and right marriage. A coward cannot own his or her shortcomings and sinful nature and deal with them. Courageous people will face reality head on and conquer their fears.

We've saved this chapter for last because, after reading the previous ones, you want intimacy. You want to be married as best friends and best lovers, but you know it's going to take guts to commit to that kind of transparency. The fear of rejection and disappointment can be overwhelming. God wants to transform your hearts to contain the quality of spirit to enable you to face fear without showing pain.

Fear can paralyze us and even compromise our ambitions. Yet courage is a commitment to continue. You may imagine a courageous person as one who is strong, confident and unmoving. What we sometimes fail to realize is that every single person in this world faces fear, and courage is never demonstrated as an absence of fear. It's more like a fighting state of spirit that says, "I see the fear, I see the hardship, and I see the challenge, yet I will overcome!" (See First John 5:3-5.)

One day I was driving to Phoenix Girls, our church Bible Study, and began flipping through the radio stations. An advertisement came on that began describing a person who was petrified of the dentist: Are you one of those people who dread going to the dentist? Do you actually avoid treatment simply out of fear? Well, we have the perfect place for you! Come to our dental office where we will happily drug you, and you will hardly remember being here, and meanwhile your teeth are fixed without any emotional trauma.

Isn't that just like our world today? Are you scared? Take a pill. Many of us avoid the treatment that we need because of fear. We're too afraid to admit our troubles to a close friend or counselor. We fear judgment and find it difficult to approach God. Most likely, we take the road of least resistance and just hope that everything will work out.

As you each confront your sins, you will be better spouses. Instead of seeing the failures in your spouse, be blatantly honest with your own heart. Stop the excuses, and face the real deal. It takes courage to admit your failures! And everything about being best friends and best lovers demands that you do! Fear will drain you of strength, cloud your judgment and rob you of joy...or it will drive you to dependence. What a safe place to be: dependent on the One who is faithful!

We love knowing our need for our heavenly Father. We love to wake up in the morning and know that it is He and only He Who satisfies us with His unfailing love. We love going to bed at night and giving Him our cares, our worries of the day, our fears and our sins. We receive everything important in life from Him. We will never be alone, unprotected or unloved; not ever. And that very attitude makes us great friends and great lovers.

It also takes courage to say "no" to self-pity. What a challenge at times! We carry much responsibility – as do you – and instead of giving in to the weariness, we must take courage and thank God for the opportunities ahead of us. The "easy way" isn't always the highest way.

We speak at many pro-life banquets and fund-raisers. First we set up the evening by describing our marriage, our life in ministry and our three children. Then we dampen the room with the news of my participation with sin and participation in an affair. Next, we talk about the choice we were faced with: Do we keep this baby? The first thing out of our doctor's mouth was, "The test came back positive. Do you want to keep the baby?"

It is then that we start unraveling the story of how we took the easy way. We see faces whiten in the room; we even hear gasps throughout the audience. As we describe our journey, we talk about what the easy way really is. We can walk down the hall to our little boy's room every night and see him sleeping soundly with his precious head on a soft pillow. We get to hear the sound of laughter day in and day out. Not only his, but the rest of us, as we enjoy his hilarious antics and his spontaneous humor. We can be in agreement with God's amazing future for his life and watch it unfold right in front of our eyes. That's the easy way. But it was not the path of least resistance.

The Holy Spirit is necessary for us to have true courage. When Jesus left the earth, He told His disciples that He was leaving them with a gift: the Holy Spirit. If you want the Holy Spirit, it is as simple as thanking God for His gift and receiving it. Ask for the whole thing. Get doused in the Holy Spirit! Receive the One who brings extreme comfort, sound teaching, wise counsel and specific leading – not to mention the gifts and the fruit!

What Did You Expect?

How do you cope with prayers that seem unanswered and a spouse who consistently and constantly disappoints? One area in which hope is often deferred between couples is that of expectations. He expects one thing and she another. Each assumes the other knows what is expected, so they never talk about it. Suddenly, both are disappointed in each other and that's when trouble starts a-brewin'.

It's never fun to disappoint the people around us. In fact, it's a downright downer! On the other side of that coin, few things are more frustrating or disheartening than to be disappointed by the people we love the most. Probably the greatest cause of disappointment in marriage is unmet expectations. The greater our expectations, the greater our disappointment when our spouse fails to live up to them. And with that failure, our disappointment can evolve very quickly into disillusionment with our marriage itself.

We all have expectations of other people; this is perfectly natural. Our expectations develop from what we are taught, from what we observe and from what we experience in life. This is why our expectations differ, for we are all different. The scary part about all this is that we seldom consciously think about our expectations, much less write them down or discuss them with anyone else, including our spouse. They are just there.

People with high expectations of others usually have similar expectations of themselves. Let's face it: If it were not for expectations, would anything get done in the world? Some expectations are good and necessary. For example, it is good for us as parents to expect proper and responsible behavior from our children. It is good for employers to communicate their expectations clearly so that their employees will perform their jobs efficiently, thoroughly and correctly.

How can someone live up to your expectations if you never voice them? And how will you know how crazy and unrealistic some of your expectations are until you say them out loud? For couples seeking to become best friends and best lovers and to learn the language of love, heart talk will include talk about expectations. What do you expect from each other personally, relationally and sexually? What are your views and expectations regarding roles and responsibilities in your relationship? What kind of behavior do you expect from your children? What are your dreams and expectations regarding family finances?

You've probably heard the saying about raising teenagers: Save the fight for the things that really matter. In other words, relax about the little things so that if and when the big issues arise you have room to talk and still maintain the respect of your children. It is the same in marriage. Once you know what your expectations are, take a vacation from the ones that aren't as important to you. Save your fight for the ones that really touch your heart. Some of your expectations are probably unrealistic.

So set aside time with your spouse to talk about your expectations, your hopes and your dreams. You both may be surprised at what you learn! Just talking about these things will bring you closer together. First of all, you are talking, and second, you will likely rediscover many of the things you have in common and the very reasons you are married! Commonalities foster closeness.

One effective way we have found for dealing with disappointment is to get in the habit of acting in the "opposite spirit." For example, when tempted by greed or selfishness, respond by giving a radical gift! Or when someone dishes out hatred or hostility, serve unconditional love in return. Acting in the opposite spirit is what Jesus meant when He said:

> ...love your enemies. Do good to those who hate you. Pray for the happiness of those who curse you. Pray for those who hurt you. If someone slaps you on one cheek, turn the other cheek. If someone demands your coat, offer your shirt also.
> Luke 6:27b-29

Another example would be asking for God's supernatural peace in the midst of confusing and hectic circumstances. With regard to disappointment, we have discovered that the "opposite spirit" is unexpected pleasures. Whenever we experience disappointment, we ask our Father in heaven for unexpected pleasures. These are like kisses from Jesus, surprises that reach beyond what I had imagined. In order to receive these, the Lord told us we needed to begin sowing them into others' lives. He promised that as we sowed them we would also reap them.

This relates directly to the process of becoming your spouse's best friend and best lover. If you have experienced disappointment, sow seeds of unexpected pleasure! Be creative, and ask God for heavenly ideas. Even if you don't see an instant rebate on this deal, you will certainly reap rewards one day. It is always a good investment to love your spouse beyond what he or she expects. It counteracts disappointment...on both sides!

Seven Aspects of the Healing Process

Take some time to meditate on these seven keys to facilitate your healing and the healing of your relationship:

Be Honest

In order to receive the final healing of God's love, I must be honest and let myself be brought to the breaking point of saying, "Yes, Lord, I need you." To the degree that I need Him, He will be there. I will receive what God wants to do, and I know that He will help me through my problem. As I become truly honest, I become truly spiritual and receive truth and grace.

Die Daily to Sin

Pain and hurt may cause me to react in a hurtful and even sinful way. When I sin, I need to remember that sin does not define me. It is not my identity. The Scripture in Romans chapter 6 lays it out well:

Verses 1-7: I have died to sin.

Verses 8-10: I know I am alive in Christ.

Verses 11-14: I am to yield myself to Christ.

Apply God's Healing Love on a Daily Basis

I will receive what is mine in Christ Jesus. There is a great inheritance, and I will live out of that. It is appropriate to receive! It's only my pride that keeps me from receiving. I will say thank you and I will gratefully acknowledge God's goodness and promises.

Encourage Relationships

Truth is an indispensable foundation for healthy relationships, and I cannot get healed unless I am held accountable for my actions. I take personal responsibility, owning what I have done, and then I receive God's forgiveness, acceptance and identity.

Meditate on the Truth

You may say, "I'm all messed up! Why?" There are three possible reasons:

I think about the things God doesn't say or believe about me.

I believe a lie.

I think about what others may or may not have said about me.

Proverbs 23:7 says, *"As a man thinketh in his heart — so is he."*

So be thankful, and think about what is true! God never intended that you be led by your emotions. That's why you must think and meditate on the truth!

6) Live by Truth, Not by Feelings

Think through the truth, meditate on it and then live it out! The truth needs to be written on the tablet of your heart. Live your life as one yielded to the Lord, for Jesus is the Truth. Be consistently honest about your feelings, and then choose righteousness!

7) Time

It takes time for healing and restoration. Ninety percent of the success is finishing. Endure through your temporary pain and win the experience of being satisfied! Experience is not the best teacher in life; evaluated experience is! Learn from your mistakes. Instead of asking, "Why?" ask, "What now?"

You Are Making a Statement

There's an advancement of the kingdom of God that needs to take place in every believer's life. When that kingdom is established, Christ says: *"But I, when I am lifted up from the earth, will draw all men to myself"* (John 12:32, NIV). Jesus gave us great instruction in the Lord's Prayer when He says, *"Thy kingdom come, Thy will be done in earth, as it is in heaven"* (Matthew 6:10, KJV). The enemy's scheme is to prevent the ruling and reigning of Christ in our marriages. If he prevents us from being effective and productive, the kingdom of God will not prevail!

The enemy is afraid when God's people rise up and become contagious and effective in their daily walk! He says, "Trust God all you want, go to church, but just don't tell others what God does in your life." The enemy hates that! When your marriage is ignited, secure and connected, what a platform to proclaim the goodness of God! There is a lost and dying world out there waiting and wanting to see the light, life and love of God being exemplified in your marriage.

Where Do I Need More Courage?

Bring God into these places of your heart. Ask Him for courage, and walk hand in hand with Him as you face your fears and conquer the unknown. Where have you taken the path of least resistance? Change gears, ask for forgiveness, receive it and move on! His mercy is new every morning, and you are receiving mercy to take the "easy way." That is the way that might mean dying to yourself today but investing in a future of pleasure, joy-filled and sprinkled with contentment, and a completely satisfied heart.

Do I Have the Holy Spirit?

Get baptized every day! Receive the power and enablement of the Holy Spirit. Let the fruit of the Holy Spirit grow in your life: love, joy, peace, patience, gentleness, goodness, faith, meekness and self-control. Admit your failures; own the sin, the mistakes and the humiliations. If God leads you, confess your sins to your spouse. Ask him or her to forgive you. Pray for courage and refuse the path of least resistance. There will be a unique and practical plan to the road of courage for every person. Write it out! We have discovered the importance of being deliberate as a married couple. We pursue each other and stay emotionally attached to each other.

There's Courage in Encouragement — Literally!

If you are facing a marriage that seems impossible at the moment, and you have made a commitment to heart transformation, you are taking a huge step in the right direction! You are laying down your own rights. Instead of fighting against your spouse, you will fight for your marriage.

There is a challenging journey ahead. Added to your courage you must find people around you who will cheer you on and believe with you for God's highest purpose in your life and marriage. If you don't have friends and family with like mind who will encourage you in your faith, find someone who will! Remember, the first rule in getting some great friends is being a great friend. You probably have friends right now who need encouragement, and you can invest in their lives. Receive encouragement from the Lord for yourself, and then begin giving out of your overflow.

As you have gained a new point of view, you are noticing qualities in your spouse that have always been there, but now you're seeing them clearly! The first person you should encourage is your spouse. Begin voicing your encouragement and hope. Your spouse certainly has characteristics and attributes that you appreciate. Declare them! Out loud!

The Search for Encouragement

God teaches us to encourage ourselves in Him! You will not have instant access to a great preacher continually! You do have access to your heavenly Father Who loves you passionately and is cheering you on in your faith by His Holy Spirit! When there is not a soul in sight who will lift you out of the depths, you still have everything you need. God will satisfy you with words of encouragement and a stimulation of hope and grace. He will walk with you every step of the way.

Hearing God's voice can be a challenge; but the Bible says that the Lord is our Shepherd, and His sheep know His voice! You may not know or recognize it, but you are hearing His voice. Listening and acknowledging His words in your heart is something you can learn and develop, and this very discipline will change your life forever!

We find that journaling our innermost thoughts and questions to Him is the most effective way to gain understanding and perspective. We cry out to Him, then listen for His voice. We write down what's in our hearts, write out Scripture passages that encourage us, and then soak in quiet moments in His presence. There is nothing more encouraging to us! It keeps us sensitive to hear Him and see Him in our moment-to-moment life. So when our little guy just says out of the blue, "Mama, I love you," or, "Daddy, you're the best daddy," or we gaze up and see the bright stars and absorb the wonder of His majesty, we see and hear beyond the physical and are seeing with our spiritual eyes that recognize the beauty and holiness of God.

As you keep your journal, you can look back and say, "Wow! I've done that before. I can take up this next challenge with the help of the Lord, and we will see victory!" Your journal time will be personal and unique for you and your relationship with God. It's a faith step to get a journal and a pen to begin. *"My heart overflows with a beautiful thought! I will recite a lovely poem to the king, for my tongue is like the pen of a skillful poet"* (Psalm 45:1).

If Others Can Do It

Another encouragement is to read about how others have pressed on. This makes us say, "Well, if they can do it, I can too!" All the people mentioned in Hebrews chapter 11 are known as heroes of the faith. They are people of God who did great exploits because they believed in God, and now they are our clouds of witnesses. Their example of perseverance and faith cheers us on and causes us to say, "We can do it too!"

Remember times when you remained faithful even though it meant terrible suffering? Sometimes you were exposed to public ridicule and were beaten, and sometimes you helped others who were suffering the same things. You suffered along with those who were thrown into jail. When all you owned was taken from you, you accepted it with joy. You knew you had better things waiting for you in eternity. Do not throw away this confident trust in the Lord, no matter what happens. Remember the great reward it brings you! Patient endurance is what you need now, so you will continue to do God's will. Then you will receive all that he has promised.

Hebrews 10:32b-36

Not one of the heroes of the faith had an easy life. They had hard choices to make, but they chose to follow the Lord. Not all of them escaped deathly circumstances and immense suffering, but that's what made them heroes. Some people won't understand your passion for marriage, especially if your spouse doesn't seem to be living up to his or her end of the bargain. They'll want to coddle you, comfort you and tell you to find a happier life. They'll see your marriage as a contract and not understand the covenant to which you are committed.

Others won't understand your confidence in the gospel. When I, Audrey, proclaim my freedom in the Lord and declare His complete forgiveness for me, there are those who rise up in judgment against me. It is human nature to throw stones at the adulterous woman. But that's not who I am. I am a daughter of the King, robed in garments of righteousness and shining in His glory. That is not arrogance, it's agreement with what Jesus has done. And what He has done for me, I am convinced He wants to do for you.

Do I let my persecutors stop me from announcing to the world that God is not holding their sins against them? Do I shrink back in shame, or do I rise up in authority that says, "I've been there, I've done that and I've seen His love and His grace"? A satisfied heart says, "There is hope for you, and we will press in and find it!" George Mueller said, "Faith starts when man's ability ends."

The days of wishy-washy prayers are over! There is power in making a decision to agree with God's truth and live in His reality for our lives. We must be deliberate and confident. It indeed is God's will for your marriage to be healed. Do not shrink back from pursuing His highest!

There Is No Room for Fear

Fear will destroy your confidence in God and keep you from owning the promises He has given you. When you make the confident decision to thrive in your marriage, there will be a temptation to ask questions like:

What if he never loves me again?

What if she betrays me?

What if he never stops punishing me?

What if God doesn't answer my prayers?

These are very real questions, and they are best dealt with from the outset. Your answer to each one lies in your relentless trust in God. You can only fully trust the One whom you really know. Get to know Him more deeply. Press in to understand His love for you. Read His Word and meditate on His promises and truth. When you really know Jesus loves you, you will trust Him no matter what comes your way.

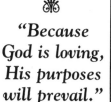

"Because God is loving, His purposes will prevail."

When your prayers aren't answered in the way you would have chosen, that is the perfect time to dig in to know God more. Holding on to Him and seeking Him despite what you see honors Him. When we really see Him for Who He is, the other things start to fade.

Our pastor, Tommy Barnett, challenges us never to start a sentence with: "If God is loving, then how come...." Instead, he has taught us to say, "Because God is loving, His purposes will prevail."

The Promised Land Marriage

When the children of Israel were ready to cross into the land of promise, Joshua said, "Fear not – be of great courage!" They were moving into the destiny that God had promised them, but it was unknown territory! There were no guarantees; all they knew was that they were following the God of covenant and promise.

You see, they had been traveling in the desert for forty years. They were going around and around, just waiting for the day when they could cross the Jordan River into the land they dreamed of. There were miracles in the desert every single day, manna falling from heaven for them to eat, water coming from a rock, a cloud leading them by day, and a pillar of fire keeping them warm every night. But they weren't satisfied, because they knew there was more.

Many of you are in marriages like that today. You're going from one miracle to the next, walking in the desert, hoping that one day there will be more. You've heard the promise, you know there's a place of fulfillment and satisfaction, but you're facing a decision: Will you cross over to the other side?

The people came to the edge of the Jordan River and faced the challenge of crossing over. They had spent forty years in the wilderness because they had refused to cross the first time. That rebellious generation was now dead, and their children were not going to make the same mistake again. The Jordan River was at its highest point; it was harvest time. It took a huge step of faith to place their feet in the Jordan. But as they did, the waters rolled back all the way to a place called Adam.

The curse is broken over your life, all the way from the beginning of mankind when Adam walked the earth. We have stepped across the Jordan and are experiencing a Promised Land marriage together, something that once we only dreamed of. We have tasted and seen that the Lord is good. We are living in the promises of God, and we are satisfied in His love. God is warring on our behalf, defeating our enemies.

You are not alone in this battle. The Lord has brought you to a place of promise where He wants you to experience abundant life to the same extent that He has possessed it and driven out the enemy before you. He has delivered him into your hands to destroy him! You are participating with what God has done already! The enemy is defeated under your feet, yet you must go and repossess what is rightfully yours. Totally destroy what has already been destroyed, those things that are no longer part of your lives. Recognize your place in His Kingdom! (See Deuteronomy chapter 7 for a full account of the children of Israel during this time.)

Hope: Confident Expectation

The land of promise awaits you. It's everything you've ever dreamed of. Fear not and take courage! Hope is the confident expectation that something good awaits you. Hang on to hope and ignite faith in your heart. It's time to soar together. You are purposed by God to be best friends and best lovers. Our prayer is that you will find joy in the journey!

> *Hope is the confident expectation that something good awaits you.*

Heart Revelation: The Tough Questions

What role does thankfulness play in our restoration? What is the opposite of thankfulness? How might dwelling on this opposite impact our Christian walk?

When have you taken the path of least resistance?

Has fear paralyzed you and compromised your ambitions?

Do you have unvoiced expectations of your spouse?

Do you need to find people around you who will cheer you on and believe with you for God's highest?

Are you willing to commit yourself to hearing God's voice every day?

Are you content to settle with an "all right" marriage, or will you press on for a Promised Land marriage?

Heart Transformation: The Truth Established

If you want the Holy Spirit, it is as simple as thanking God for the gift and receiving it. Ask for the whole thing – get baptized in the Holy Spirit! (See Acts 1-2.)

I want to make "responding in the opposite spirit" a way of life! (See Galatians 5:24.)

I will let the fruit of the Holy Spirit grow out of my life: love, joy, peace, patience, gentleness, goodness, faith, meekness and self-control. (See Galatians 5:22.)

I have access to my heavenly Father Who loves me passionately and is cheering me on in my faith! (See Luke 11:13.)

There is power in making a decision to agree with God's truth and to live in His reality for our lives. (See John 14:15-21.)

Prayer

Thank You, Father, that the Holy Spirit is a gift to those who ask! It is the Holy Spirit that we feel...and we must feel to believe. Lord, I allow my feelings to get wrapped up in Your comfort, Your embrace, Your touch, Your longing for me. I'm so thankful that I don't have to do one thing to make myself irresistible to You, for You love me with an everlasting love.

His Response

Your Father in heaven wants to give you back your smile. If you're all alone right now, take a moment to close your eyes and smile back at Him. He's smiling at you, and is reassuring you of His acceptance. There is no reason to feel guilty any longer. There's no reason to hide. As you have received His forgiveness, He has cleansed you completely and made you pure. His grace has enabled you to live life with Him. He will never leave you or forsake you.

Receive your inheritance! His hope, His grace, His enablement!

Prayer

Lord, I am thankful for all Your promises and I receive absolutely everything You have for me and for my marriage. Thank You for calling me Your own.

Soaring Together: God Was Pursuing Them

He was a police officer and she was a nurse. They had beautiful young children...and a broken marriage. After years of dysfunction, with both having affairs and punishing one another, they were on the road to divorce, already living in separate homes. He went to work one day and one of his colleagues told him about an interview he had seen on television in which a couple, Bob and Audrey, spoke about marriage. He shrugged it off.

The next day, he was flipping channels and caught part of the interview on a repeat station. He couldn't shrug off the coincidence. He emailed us in an attempt to gain perspective. He purchased *Marriage Under Cover* and began reading the story of how God had moved in our marriage in miracles, bringing hope in the midst of impossible circumstances. He gave the book to his wife.

Two months later, both quite uneasy, they attended a marriage retreat together where we were speaking. We met with them and prayed together with them. They both gave their lives to the Lord and then proceeded to face each other. They looked deep into each other's eyes and God's grace began to flow. The presence of God entered their relationship and they have never looked back! They sold one house, moved in together, began attending church and are now sharing their testimony with others. The best part of all is the smiles on their faces, and the fact that their children and future generations are saved from the ravages of divorce! This couple is drop-dead gorgeous – gleaming with joy and ignited with passion and purpose. They are world changers!

WHAT OTHERS ARE SAYING ABOUT MARRIAGE UNDER COVER

These few comments represent thousands of readers who have responded to our story. From pastors to professionals to counselors and couples, *Marriage Under Cover* is being used as a tool to bring hope to the multitudes!

Alberta, Canada

Thank you for your book. My divine appointment came this weekend. Once I began to read it I could not put it down until it was finished. For so many years betrayal has been there. In this past 20 years I have come to recognize all betrayal as being our stepping away from God's love and grace. It is always that relationship that I must come back to.

The God gift of love and grace in your book and story was quite unexpected. Sharing what you went through was like salve on these hidden wounds, questions that could be answered. Not only have you freed yourself and shown the power of believing in God's love instead of betrayal, you are freeing others by sharing your journey. I felt waves of understanding and compassion come over me and God's love and grace embraced me. I thank you for sharing God's love and grace with me and my family. Truly with God all things are possible. Thank you.

Seattle, Washington

My counselor asked me to read *Marriage Under Cover*. After reading your story I feel so free. My greatest challenge was forgiving myself for the affair I had. My husband and I read the book together and shed so many tears. I think my husband let it all go after holding it all inside for the past two years. We are just overflowing with joy; it's hard to contain. We went to our church this past Sunday and told our pastor about what happened this past weekend, and he would like us to give our testimony when we feel ready. We both feel like the Lord is leading us to reach out to other couples and help them as they go through similar situations. Life just feels so great right now; I never knew we could be full of joy again. Thank you for giving us hope for a wonderful future together. God is so good!

Denver, Colorado

I just finished your book *Marriage Undercover*, and I can tell you that it is helping me a lot. I will be going through the book with my husband as well. I have just been through something similar and so much of what you have written about the feelings and deceit is so accurate. I had felt that I was the only one going through this. Then your book tells me that you had exactly the same feelings that I did....Wow!

I know this will be a rough road ahead and I know that God will be with me the entire way. I just want to thank you and your husband for having the courage and taking the time to write a book that will be a help to other couples. Bless you for that.

I pray for the strength to get through the daily battles in this war. My husband is a brand new Christian and I had fallen away from the Lord. Now I am home in His house and we are all going through this together. Thanks again for your book. I am in a small town and with the exception of our pastor, spiritual counseling is limited, especially on this subject...

Richmond, Virginia

Thank you for being a light on the steps of my life. I have searched for love from a high school boyfriend miles away to fill the void only God can fill. I struggle daily with the temptation to receive a small bit of attention and caring from a man from my past. Your honesty and transparency have given me hope to win my spiritual warfare with the strength of a loving heavenly Father. Thank you. May God bless your ministry in ways you never expected. Praise God! I just can't tell you how much it blessed me! My husband and I have been married for 12 years. We have a wonderful past steeped in the promise that God has big plans for us and desires to use us for His glory. We both went to school at Oral Roberts University. We both had wonderful relationships with leaders in that community and were mentored by some wonderful Christian leaders. Our journey together had "engine needs service" warnings big time in spite of our rich mentoring and relationships. We have a brand new, clean, miraculous, victorious, and wonderful marriage! We also can attest to the fact that nothing is too difficult for Christ! We are so grateful for new life! I love my husband! He really, really, really, loves me! God has given us life! Thank you for sharing your story! It gave me reason to rejoice again! Thank you.

Detroit, Michigan

We have been hurting so badly. We went to see our pastor, and he suggested we read *Marriage Under Cover*. I was really touched...tears filled my eyes. When things seem impossible for us, God makes them possible! My husband and I went through a similar situation. I praise the Lord because He helped us through and we're still standing. Thank you for being so honest. We feel understood, and knowing that you have made it to the other side just keeps us going!

Phoenix, Arizona

I picked up your book, *Marriage Under Cover*, on Monday, March 20. I was looking in the marriage section of my local bookstore because I'd had an affair and I was struggling with the decision of whether to tell my husband or not. So I picked up your book, and I was immediately drawn to the dedication on the inside; it was truly a divine appointment. As I began reading the book, I realized that I felt the same way as you on many things. I grew up in a Christian home. I'm happy in my marriage. My husband and I are in ministry together. But I let one thought lead to another and it enticed me. It's now the afternoon of Wednesday, March 22 and I've nearly read the whole book. I told my husband about my affair last night. He questioned me a lot, then left for a while, but he came home and slept in the same bed with me. I am very thankful for that. He said he loves me and wants to work things out, but he doesn't know how it will happen at this point. This is harder than I thought it would be. Usually when you confess your sins, you feel better and there is forgiveness. I feel better that it's out in the open, but it's so painful to face the reality of the road ahead.

I am writing to thank you for telling your story. I pray that one day we will be able to use our story for the glory of God as well.

Philippines

We are missionaries here in the Philippines. I was truly blessed to see your hearts and to see how God has fully redeemed the situation. He is so awesome! Of course sin can never be justified. But when it does happen to a believer or even a minister, it's not the sin that defines that person, but it's what he or she does after being confronted that shows who they really are. In the Word, we see both negative examples (Judas went out and hanged himself, Pilate "washed his hands" of his sin), and positive examples (both David and Peter wept and repented when they were exposed). Clearly, you both have chosen a positive track and God is blessing your lives.

I have seen many interviews on Christian TV, but never have I seen one as compelling as Joni's interviews with you. You guys have guts. I think it's awesome that you were so open and honest about the whole situation. I believe those TV interviews, as well as your book and your ongoing ministry, will help millions of people, both among the saved and the unsaved. Every aspect of your story...the repentance, the way both of you dealt with your initial reactions to it and fought through the pain with godly counsel, the decision to stay together, the forgiveness, the initial effort not to spread the news to those who didn't need to know, the way you rejected the abortion option once learning of the pregnancy, the way you shared the news with your children, the new start through a move to a new city and country, the birth of Robert and the naming of him after Bob so he would know he is loved (that part was awesome!), and finally your complete transparency with the world and the body of Christ in sharing the story so others can be helped . . . all of it . . . has been done so right. It's inspiring. Two wrongs never make a right, but a lot of rights can go a long way to wiping out the pain and shame of a wrong. And, of course, a sin repented of is as far as the east is from the west, according to the Lord.

Well done, Bob and Audrey! You have allowed Jesus to shine through your lives in the fullness of the Redeemer that He truly is.

Australia

My Dad gave me a copy of your book last Friday. I was completely absorbed in your story from cover to cover! I read a lot and I have never written to the author of any book before, but I feel compelled to thank both you and Bob for being so courageous and honest in sharing your story. Your story has touched my heart and soul and I thank God for you both....your story has been such a blessing to me and to my husband!

Well, thank you for taking the time to read this email. I see on your web site that you are visiting Australia late this year (that's were I am!), so I will look forward to hearing both you and Bob speak.

ABOUT THE AUTHORS

As accomplished authors, international speakers and television hosts, Bob and Audrey Meisner are currently hosting the television program *It's a New Day*, seen daily across Canada and internationally through the Internet at www.newday.org. Passionate about marriage, they speak to the lives and hearts of couples through conferences around the world.

Their first book together, *Marriage Under Cover*, quickly became a best-seller and has been featured on some of the nation's top Christian television programs. Noted for their honest depiction of adultery that led to an unexpected pregnancy, they are ambassadors of hope in the midst of pain and declarers of truth about triumphant thriving in seemingly impossible situations.

Bob and Audrey are experienced as producers and writers of *Sonshiny Day*, a television program geared toward young children which has aired internationally and has been translated into various languages. They have pioneered and pastored a church and Bob is an ordained minister. The Meisners live together in Phoenix, Arizona with their four children.

To contact the Meisners, please visit www.BobandAudrey.com.

ABOUT THE BOOK

This is a true story that every husband and wife should read. Bob and Audrey Meisner had it all: a fruitful ministry, three beautiful children, a "picture-perfect" marriage. Their future seemed secure and their prospects bright—until adultery threatened to bring it all crashing down. Faced with the greatest personal crisis of their lives, Bob and Audrey found hope and rescue through godly counsel and through learning the biblical principle of covering to protect their marriage and their family.

Through heart-wrenching emotional anguish, deep layers of repentance and forgiveness, and even an unanticipated pregnancy, Bob and Audrey found restoration in discovering the true nature of supernatural love and the limitless grace of a merciful God. Against all conventional "wisdom" and human expectations, their marriage not only survived, but came to thrive in the midst of a culture that is increasingly hostile to traditional family values.

Learn how to cover your marriage and protect your family. Rediscover how to become irresistible to your spouse. Learn how to make your marriage thrive in a culture of quiet desperation.

Take cover! Don't leave your marriage unprotected!

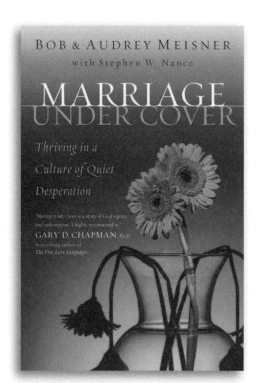

About the Authors

Bob and Audrey Meisner are co-hosts of the television program, It's A New Day, seen daily across Canada and the U.K. Individually and as a couple, they have been working in Christian television since 1984. Having pioneered in broadcasting and church planting, Bob and Audrey are now popular marriage conference speakers. Together they are committed to communicating God's love to a hurting world. They are passionate about marriages being everything God designed them to be. The Meisners currently live in Winnipeg, Manitoba with their three teenagers and a three-year-old.

Marriage Undercover
by Bob & Audrey Miesner
ISBN 0-924748-45-1 • UPC 88571300015-4
Retail $13.99 • 224 pages • Trade

"Marriage Under Cover is a story of God's grace and redemption. I highly recommend it."
Gary D. Chapman, Ph.D.
Best-selling author of *The Five Love Languages*

NOTES